2678
9.78

the CORE

REALITIES OF YOUTH MINISTRY

NINE BIBLICAL PRINCIPLES
THAT MARK HEALTHY
YOUTH MINISTRIES

MIKE YACONELLI

with commentary by the entire CORE training team—
Dave Ambrose, Les Christie, Heather Flies,
Megan Hutchinson, Dan Jessup, Tic Long, Fred Lynch,
Helen Musick, Mark Oestreicher, Marv Penner,
Laurie Polich, Duffy Robbins, Charley Scandlyn, Efrem Smith

Youth Specialties

ZONDERVAN™

GRAND RAPIDS, MICHIGAN 49530 USA

WWW.ZONDERVAN.COM

Youth Specialties

The CORE Realities of Youth Ministry: Nine Biblical Principles That Mark Healthy Youth Ministries
Copyright © 2003 Youth Specialties.

Youth Specialties Books, 300 South Pierce Street, El Cajon, CA 92020, are published by Zondervan, 5300 Patterson Aveune SE, Grand Rapids, MI 49530

Library of Congress Cataloging-in-Publication Data

Yaconelli, Mike.
   The CORE realities of youth ministry : nine biblical principles that
mark healthy youth ministries / by Mike Yaconelli.
      p. cm.
   ISBN 0-310-25513-9 (pbk.)
   1. Church work with youth. I. Title.
   BV4447.Y25 2004
   259'.23--dc22

                                                                200301460

Edited by Sally Harris
Cover and interior design by Brian Smith
Printed in the United States of America

05 06 07 /   / 10 9 8 7 6

Contents

Introduction:
The CORE Realities
of Youth Ministry

Congratulations! You wouldn't be reading this book if you hadn't received the greatest calling any person could receive—the call to youth ministry. Whether you are on staff or a volunteer, old or young, fat or skinny, cool or uncool, God has chosen you, which means he has his hand on you. By responding to God's call to youth ministry, we have committed to go in whatever direction God wants to take us: east, west, right, left, up, down, and even sometimes upside down. Youth ministry is one unbelievable roller-coaster ride!

We won't always know where God is going to take us, but we can try to prepare ourselves for those wild rides. As youth ministers, we should try to understand where we began, where we are, and how we can best do God's work with what we are given. In this book, we give you some information that can help with this. First, though, we want to say a bit about some important concepts in youth ministry.

Youth ministry has been the church's response to the crisis of a generation of students who find themselves caught in the current of culture. Culture is not evil, but neither is it neutral. Because of the effect their culture was having on teenagers a number of years ago, the church realized youth needed specialized attention, so youth ministry was created to help them develop the resources to survive this culture as children of God.

It is unclear exactly who invented the concept of youth ministry, and it is possible that a group of adults who were concerned about the students in their area gathered in a local church and said, "We need to do something for the youth; they need help." Many people say, though, that the concept of youth ministry was developed by Torrey Johnson, an evangelist in the 1940s. Others credit Jim Rayburn, the founder of Young Life, who said youth ministry is not difficult; it is simply *an adult building a relationship with a student.* Really, though, it doesn't matter who invented youth ministry. Rayburn noted what really matters: youth ministry is about relationships—with teenagers and with Jesus.

At the heart of youth ministry in the church is a commitment to Jesus and to students, and the word we use for this commitment to youth is "calling." A **calling** is a holy attraction, an involuntary tugging, an unshakable sense that you can't do anything else. A person cannot be appointed, obligated, or manipulated into doing youth work; he or she must be called. Your calling may have shown up after you volunteered to help with the youth group. Maybe you raised your hand to go to the bathroom during a church board meeting on the crisis of students, and now you are in charge. Maybe your calling felt like an obligation or a feeling you should do more. Our calling can show up when our children leave the house for college, while we are chaperoning a youth event, or when we are overwhelmed with boredom.

There are many different ways we hear our calling, but there is no doubt how the calling feels. We fall in love with the teenagers, and we find ourselves enjoying their company—actually *liking* being with them—and as we spend time with them, we discover a godly connection that becomes the foundation of a relationship with these students, a relationship we never expected. These relationships develop differently for each of us. Some of us find it easy to talk to students, to hang out with them, and to do things with them; others find talking difficult and discover the power of being with students, listening quietly, paying attention to them and their world. Our callings may be unique, but there is one aspect that is a part of every calling to youth ministry: *when we do youth work, we feel God's pleasure.*

Youth ministry is all about relationship and calling, but it does have other aspects. One of these is the program. **Program** is what we do with teenagers. Some programs are large, complex, and active with youth meetings, Bible studies, special events, mission trips, concerts, and evangelistic outreach. Others are modest and intimate with small meetings once a week and an occasional camp thrown in during the year. The content of a program depends on a number of factors such as the size of the group, the amount of time the youth worker has available, the facilities, and the budget. Whatever our resources, there are hundreds of books and products available to help us find creative ways to program.

In addition to programming, another important aspect of youth work is a philosophy of ministry. **Philosophy** is not about what we do with students; it is about *why we do what we do*. It is a fancy word for *foundation*, the core beliefs that explain, drive, and define our youth ministries. Because we are the church, we base our core beliefs on Scripture.

This book is about the core beliefs of youth ministry. We call them **CORE realities**. In this book, we focus on one CORE foundation and nine CORE realities. There are nine instead of 12 or 15 because we believe these particular realities are critical for this generation of students. At the beginning of each chapter that addresses a CORE reality, we list a number of Bible verses on which we base that reality. After all, the Bible is our CORE foundation. The nine CORE realities are not exhaustive, nor are they meant to be prescriptive—they are meant to be *illuminating*. As we place our youth ministries under the light of these realities, we should discover practical implications that will help our ministries become more effective. Of course, we believe there is more than one way to do ministry, so we're not asking you to do youth ministry the way we do it. We do believe, however, that these CORE realities will help you do youth ministry *the way you do it…only better*. They can help shape our ministries to make significant differences in the teenagers God has given us.

As we work with these students, there is one thing we must remember: *youth ministry is not about us; it's about God.* It is very easy for us to lose our bearings and believe that we are in control, that our ministries depend upon our programs, our talents, our dazzling ideas. They don't. No one—not Youth Specialties, not anyone else—has all the answers, but we all have some knowledge and experience. We hope the CORE realities discussed in this book will add to your knowledge about youth ministry.

CHAPTER ONE

CORE FOUNDATION

THE BIBLE

Mike's Story

I began this wild ride called youth ministry 42 years ago. Armed with a few communication skills, no experience, and a passion for God, I jumped into ministry feet first. For reasons I can't explain, I intuitively knew I had access to what was most important—my Bible. Although I was kicked out of both Bible colleges I attended, something (or Someone) convinced me that the words written in this book were more than important—they were critical! As it turned out, the words of God kept me on the trail of God. And he is on my trail.

Looking back over the years, I realize the Bible isn't magic, but it is corrective; it isn't an answer book, it is a living book; it isn't a fix-it book, it is relationship book. When I confront God's word, I am confronted; when I read God's word, it reads me; when I seek God's presence, he seeks me. The Bible has woven its way into my heart, soaked into my bones, given direction, provided hope, and demanded humility. It has been a companion along the way—a friend and a mentor. After four decades of use, it is still fresh, still relevant, and still full of life-giving truth.

So when I do youth ministry, I just grab my Bible, jump into God's arms, and hang on for the ride.

Because the CORE realities are founded on the truths of Scripture, it's important that we spend some time focusing on the Bible and understanding the role of Scripture in our ministries. Obviously, we don't worship the Bible; we worship the God of the Bible, and it is the Bible that tells us about God. It helps us develop our relationship with God, guides us in our relationships with others, and reveals the truth for us today—here and now.

Even though the Bible was written thousands of years ago, it's still relevant today. We believe the truths of the Bible are unchanging, but the implications of truth change continually as culture and teenagers change. This generation of students is like every generation in some ways and unlike every generation in other ways. That's why we trust the Bible—it speaks to both realities: the unchanging human condition and the constantly changing cultural conditions. It speaks to all generations.

We trust the Bible because it's the truth. It was the truth when it was written, and it is the truth now. It's the truth now because it's living truth. In our lives, the word of God acts; it affects us and lives with us. God's words are the breath of life, a mystery, and a story. They live, reveal, interfere, inspire, and provide a solid foundation. These are just eight of the many characteristics of biblical truth, and below are the ways in which these characteristics affect us. These, we believe, are the foundations of the CORE realities.

1. Biblical Truth is God-breathed.

All Scripture is God-breathed and is useful for teaching, rebuking, correcting and training in righteousness....

(2 Timothy 3:16)

Timothy says that the words in the Bible emanate from God, like the very breath of God, the wind of God. These words can help train us in righteousness. By reading God's words, we can know the mysteries of God; we can know what God is up to.

Hold on. Before we get too excited, it's important to remember the words of God in Isaiah:

"For my thoughts are not your thoughts, neither are your ways my ways," declares the Lord.
"As the heavens are higher than the earth, so are my ways higher than your ways and my thoughts than your thoughts." (55:8-9)

Even though God's words are directly from him, we won't always know specifically what God is up to. God's words can teach, rebuke, correct, and train. They also can confuse and amaze. They draw us to the shores of mystery....

2. Biblical Truth is a mystery.

Pray also for me, that whenever I open my mouth, words may be given me so that I will fearlessly make known the mystery of the gospel.

(Ephesians 6:19)

The Bible is filled with awe-inspiring mystery. This mystery is part of our delight in God's word. Our goal in youth ministry, then, is to educate teenagers in the Scriptures and to show them the mystery, to render them speechless by what they read. We want them to be literate as well as astonished, surprised, shocked, spellbound, overwhelmed, and awestruck. We want them to find answers, and we want them to meet the God beyond answers. When Jesus met the disciples on the water (Matthew 14, Mark 6, John 6), they were terrified. Talk about drama and mystery! The disciples were frightened out of their minds...and intrigued. Jesus knew the power of the mysterious. As well as teaching his disciples, Jesus scared the sandals off them. By walking on the water, he terrified the disciples—they thought he was a ghost! Reading about the Son of God walking on the water can cause us to experience terror as well. Our task is to introduce students to the terrifying power of the Savior through the biblical story.

In my middle school days, we were herded into the gym for ballroom dancing class. Talk about torture! Coach Welch had a knack for making a waltz feel like calisthenics: "Hut-two-three-slide!" All the while, though, he kept telling us how graceful this was, how wonderful, how romantic. I remember thinking, "I wish this girl would just leave me alone and let me get these stupid steps right!"

But little did we realize that ballroom dancing is not simply about getting the steps right—it's about a growing relationship with your partner, about moving together in an embrace of openness and developing intimacy. It's about the mysterious connection that enables you to dance beautifully.

Often we imply that true spirituality is about getting "the steps" of the dance right. Except that the Bible doesn't give us "five easy steps to a happy life" or "four easy steps to wonderful children" or "three easy steps to a pain-free existence." But the mystery of the gospel is that God calls us to seek his face, to read his Word, to develop that growing intimacy—and in the mystery of that relationship, we will find we are moving in unison with him.

—*Duffy Robbins*

3. Biblical Truth is a story.

The Bible is not primarily a proof text or a doctrinal statement; it is a drama. It is not only theology; it is a poem. It is not only facts; it is an adventure. The biblical story is a captivating read that should leave us breathless. In

> Let's not be so concerned about making sure the Bible is completely understood all the time. If I simplify the incredible mystery of Scripture to the point where an adolescent mind (or an adult one, for that matter) can fully grasp it, I reduce the author to my level. Because if God is God, his word will, by definition, be beyond me. Kids today are much more comfortable with this than most adults.
>
> —*Dave Ambrose*

fact, Hebrews 11 retells the events of the Old Testament as a story. Ultimately, this story is a *love* story, and this love story is made up of a collection of stories that point teenagers to the storyteller, the lover.

This story of truth and love, according to Psalm 119, is invigorating, sensual, terrifying, colorful, comforting, disturbing, visual, convicting, and penetrating. Woo hoo! It does more than stimulate our thinking; it exposes our very hearts, thoughts, desires, and passions; it defines sin; it convicts us of sin; it clarifies virtue and integrity—we read it, and it reads us!

Most people are anxious to hear the truth, and God help those who kill that expectancy by making the Bible boring. Sadly, many of us can remember attending a church, Sunday school, or youth group where our expectancy

> It's no secret that adolescents today are predisposed to experiencing life as a series of intersecting stories. Students' identities are found in the complex relational and circumstantial plots of their formative years. "You will know me if you take the time to get to know my story" is their invitation. And one thing that makes Scripture attractive to this generation is that it's a fascinating story in which they have a role. If I can introduce them to a script in which their personal stories are written, they can embrace the relevance of Scripture.
>
> —*Marv Penner*

was smothered. Mark 10 and Luke 18 say the children ran toward Jesus. They wouldn't be kept from him; even the disciples couldn't keep the children away. They wanted to learn about God. Our youth groups are filled with "children" like these who are anxious to sit at Christ's feet and hear the story.

Yet there's a kind of antitheological bias in current youth ministry culture. It says, "Don't give me theology; just give me Jesus." But talking about Jesus requires theological understanding. That's why Scripture also explores doctrinal themes in books like Romans, James, and Hebrews. The Bible is a combination of stories and statements.

—*Duffy Robbins*

4. Biblical Truth is alive.

For the word of God is living and active. Sharper than any double-edged sword, it penetrates even to dividing soul and spirit, joints and marrow; it judges the thoughts and attitudes of the heart.

(Hebrews 4:12)

The writer of Hebrews believes that God's story is "living and active." The Bible isn't dead, reduced to a list of statements or doctrines or theological principles. *It is alive!* We don't just hear truth; we taste it, smell it, touch it, wrestle with it, argue with it, confront it, turn away from it, hide from it, hold it, and fall in love with it. It is more than intellectual—it is sensual. The mystics memorized the Scriptures, said them aloud over and over again, until the words of God became a part of them, flowed through them like water, soaking into their skin and bones—until Scripture became like an old friend.

"Some people can memorize Scripture, but I just can't." How many times have we heard that from our students, our coworkers…or from our own lips? When we are confronted with temptation, despair, pain, persecution, loneliness, doubts, or fear, being able to speak the very words of the Bible to our hearts and souls is a gift. "Praying the Scriptures" on a daily basis, not only with the Bible open but with it closed as well, is one of the more intimate encounters we can have with Jesus. I've never met students (or adults) who didn't have hundreds of pop songs memorized—shouldn't we be at least as connected to Scripture?

—*Dan Jessup*

5. Biblical Truth reveals and identifies.

Nothing in all creation is hidden from God's sight. Everything is uncovered and laid bare before the eyes of him to whom we must give account.

(Hebrews 4:13)

Following this writer's description of the living power of God's word in 4:12, this verse is a bit humiliating; it says that *God sees us naked.* No pretending. No illusions. The Bible does more than speak to us, though; it penetrates our hearts and our souls. Because it is alive and has a mysterious power to penetrate us, we cannot hide anything from it.

God's word not only exposes us, showing us naked before him, it also reveals who we are. It provides a litany of names for us: names that define us, names that call us, names that strengthen and empower us. The Bible tells us who we are in the midst of a hostile world (aliens, strangers) and who we are in the midst of his kingdom (chosen, a royal priesthood, a holy nation). More importantly, it names us as "a people belonging to God." We are his children, heirs with Christ, more than conquerors—*we are his beloved.* When

"Loser!" "Lazy!" "Slut!" "Stupid!" By the time many students reach early adolescence, they've heard these words yelled at them thousands of times. That leads to some really distorted and inaccurate conclusions about who they are—and left unchallenged, they become the basis for a distorted adult identity. The good news is that God's Word communicated through caring adults is the most effective way to challenge their negative self-perceptions. Scripture has the power to give kids a whole new set of names, and we must be consciously committed to introducing our students to the words defining who they are in Christ.

—*Marv Penner*

the world without God says we are irrelevant, worthless, and narrow-minded losers, we can hold our heads high because the word of God says we are beloved. When others criticize, demean, and diminish us, we don't have to fight back; we can rest in our identity in Christ. When we stand completely exposed by biblical truth, we are revealed as his beloved.

6. Biblical Truth interferes and instructs.

The Bible disturbs and interferes because it is filled with new information: new ways of looking at life, new ways of approaching relationships, new ways of living with our neighbors, new ways of treating the poor, new ways of acting toward our enemies. This new way of thinking interferes with the status quo. It forces us to revaluate, to rethink, to revise how we live our lives.

God's word lives with us in the trenches, getting its hands dirty and interfering with our lives. It confronts, intimidates, and irritates us. *Intimidate* and *irritate* are ugly words, but they are part of the way biblical truth interferes with our lives. Intimidation invades, threatens, annoys, and inflames. And what makes the word of God invaluable is the intimidating quality of truth. The Bible speaks the truth even when we would rather not hear it. That is irritating. God's word makes us feel good, and it makes us feel bad. When our behavior is biblically challenged, when Scripture informs it, it means our lives are constantly open to change; our behavior is always in process, always being revived.

Timothy's words in 2 Timothy 3:16, "rebuking, correcting and training," are all about change, about learning how to do things in a new way, about correcting and altering our course, even while we're on course. When a momma bird pushes her little chick out of the nest, she's *training*. This kind of training interferes with our lives of contentment. We're not talking about a nice comfortable classroom where the lessons can be learned in safety and written on a blackboard; we're talking about being pushed unwillingly out of the nest, plunging toward our death, and being forced to use wings we didn't know we had—that is biblical instruction.

7. Biblical Truth inspires.

As it interferes with our lives, confronting and challenging us, the Bible also motivates, encourages, and affirms us. It brings us to new heights and places we never thought we'd go. It causes us to do things we never thought we would do, motivates us when we want to give up, and gives us courage when we are afraid. It inspires us. It ignites our passion for God.

When something is ignited, old, lifeless material is set on fire. What was just wrinkled and dull becomes a hot, exploding, consuming fire. In the same way, the Bible transforms us, gives us life when we are dead, and

The prophet Jeremiah knew the power of the ever-present word of God. In between messages of gloom, he was able to say, "When your words came, I ate them; they were my joy and my heart's delight" (15:16). This image of "eating" God's word shows us that taking it into our hearts, even in the most difficult times, provides us with the nourishment we need to survive; it inspires us to continue.

—*Laurie Polich*

creates passion in us when there is none. The word of God sets people on fire, captivates them, and fills them with enthusiasm, energy, and passion. When we have this passion, we can do amazing things. The words of God inspire us to climb to unexpected heights.

8. Biblical Truth is a trustworthy foundation.

I will show you what he is like who comes to me and hears my words and puts them into practice. He is like a man building a house, who dug down deep and laid the foundation on rock. When a flood came, the torrent struck that house but could not shake it, because it was well built. But the one who hears my words and does not put them into practice is like a man who built a house on the ground without a foundation. The moment the torrent struck that house, it collapsed and its destruction was complete.
(Luke 6:47-49)

This is the key question for this generation of students: *Is the Bible trustworthy?* They want to experience the Bible, to try it out, to put their weight on it, which is the meaning of *trust* in Hebrew. Our job is to show kids that God's word can be trusted to work in their lives, that it is rock-solid.

In Psalm 19:7 David writes, "The law of the Lord is perfect, reviving the soul. The statutes of the Lord are trustworthy, making wise the simple."

The Hebrew word for law is *Torah*, literally translated "throw the rock." It points to an ancient practice used by travelers when walking along nighttime roads. When they reached an uncertain stretch of road, they threw a rock and listened for its landing. If they heard it hit the ground ahead, they knew it was safe. If they heard a splash, there was a body of water ahead. If they heard no sound, a cliff was probably nearby. If they heard a voice, they knew an angry pedestrian was approaching. Throwing the rock, Torah, helped travelers find their way in the dark.

What a privilege to tell our kids that there is a Rock they can listen for; that there is a Word that's a lamp unto their feet and a light unto their paths—that the statutes of the Lord are trustworthy.

—*Duffy Robbins*

We can't make them believe the Bible, but we know that if and when they put their weight on it, they will realize it holds them. Some of us were 25, 35, or even older before we put our weight on it. But it held us! Which is why we are in youth ministry—*we know the Bible is a trustworthy foundation; it does what it says and it endures all types of stormy weather.*

CORE foundation: The Bible

Because the Bible is a trustworthy foundation, is the living word of God, and affects our lives daily, our interactions with teenagers should be saturated in Scripture. We should teach, memorize, and reference Scripture constantly. If the words of God are alive, if his word can interact with us, then we need to revive the art of pondering Scripture. When Mary was caught in the whirlwind of giving birth to the Messiah and constantly being interrupted by shepherds and wise men, Luke 2:19 tells us that Mary "treasured all these things and pondered them in her heart." This means she listened, valued, savored, and cherished the word of God while she waited patiently. Too many of us rush the power of Scripture—we want instant transformation and instant answers, but sometimes the word of God takes time to work. It's often working even when it doesn't look like it's working. Of course we want students to trust God's words, but first, *we need to trust his words, treasuring and pondering them.* Then we need to give space to the Holy Spirit who, slowly and determinedly, can nurture biblical Truth in our lives and the lives of our students.

The preceding list of characteristics of Biblical Truth is not complete, but it gives you a number of reasons why Scripture is the foundation of the CORE realities and why it must be treasured and pondered. The word of God is alive and well. It is the Truth, and it is a lamp, a guide, an anchor we can trust in the midst of our current cultural storm.

CHAPTER TWO

CORE REALITY

VERACITY

JOHN 1:1-3; 8:32; 14:6; 16:13-14, 21

I TIMOTHY 2:15, 13

2 JOHN 3-4; 21

2 CORINTHIANS 2:14-16

PSALM 43:3

Mike's Story

As director of a junior high camp, I thought it would be hilarious if one of the head counselors and I scared the junior high girls who had just settled down after lights out. Dressed as Frankenstein, Jim Kenagy, a very large man, stood on a bluff above the girls' dorm making noises, holding a large rock, and marching stiff-legged toward the dorm. I shined a flashlight on him and yelled, "Hey, who are you? Get out of here!" Jim and I had a hard time trying not to laugh. This was funny.

It hadn't occurred to us that junior high girls crowded into a just-darkened dormitory, staying in an unfamiliar place, and awakened from a sound sleep might not think it was funny, that they might become hysterical. We had never witnessed true junior-high-school-girl hysteria—until now.

The screaming began. At first it was sporadic, and then it spread. Most of the girls had not even seen Jim's Frankenstein; they responded to the hysteria of those who had or, rather, thought they had. Soon the screaming turned into crying. Girls passed out in the hallways; others tried to escape through the emergency exit doors; and one girl, completely out of control, smashed her arm through the window of her room.

A retired nurse and widow, Mae volunteered to work at this camp for the summer because she loved junior high kids and because she loved Jesus. Even though she was a sweet, kind old woman over 65, she was tough. Being summoned to calm hysterical girls frightened by their camp leaders did not please her. When the girls had calmed down and the wounds were bound, Mae spoke with us...no, actually she spoke to us.

I'll never forget that talk. It was magic. As she marched around the room, Mae voiced her anger, disappointment, disgust, shock, righteous indignation, sadness, and disillusionment. She ended her 20-minute reprimand with a call to remember our mission: to care for these children—for their souls—and to show them Jesus. Then she stopped. The silence was agonizing.

When I finally mustered the courage to look up, I realized Mae was smiling; she was laughing. As she left the room, Mae winked.

Mae Miller was a godly combination of passion, integrity, honesty, and fun because she walked in the truth. Mae Miller was a woman of veracity.

In his third epistle John says, "I have no greater joy than to hear that my children are walking in the truth" (1:4). They, like Mae, were people of veracity; they *conformed to the truth and walked in the truth.* We don't use the word *veracity* very often because it sounds distant, obscure, and philosophical, but it isn't. Veracity gets its hands dirty—it is truth being lived, expressed by what we do. It describes the incarnation: the truth abiding with us, in the flesh.

Through his actions Jesus showed us how to conform to the truth, and the many names he was given can help us see what veracity looks like: a friend, a shepherd, the living water, and the way. As a friend, his truth builds relationships, intimacy, trust, and community. As a shepherd, his truth disciplines, protects, and guides us. As the living water, his truth quenches our thirsts, passions, hungers, and desires. As the way, his truth directs our lives. Jesus lived a life walking in the truth so that others might see and believe.

Likewise, our youth ministries should conform to the truth. As youth workers, not only must we speak the truth, we must walk in it. It should be reflected in every part of our youth programs, from the camps to the counseling. Walking in truth does not mean we know all of the truth, but it does mean we try to conform to the truth we know. When we do this, when we (and our programs) have veracity, teenagers can glimpse what Christianity might look like in *their* lives. When students see adults trying to live the Christian faith, then they can begin living it, too. Most importantly, if teenagers can catch a whiff of the fragrance of truth, they will be attracted to it and become people of veracity.

What veracity looks like in people's lives varies tremendously. There are, though, some aspects that are always evident, things people will always see when they encounter a person who is walking in the truth. Here are just a few of those aspects.

Veracity shows that Truth is free.

Then you will know the truth, and the truth will set you free.
(John 8:32)

Truth flourishes in freedom. Rather than being locked in a prison or a tiny room that keeps it from life, God's truth roams free, getting into every aspect of life. When we walk in truth, we, too, become free. It releases us to the real world, to God's world. This freedom means that our lives are challenged; we are given blessings and responsibilities. In our lives, freedom means we are not afraid of untruth, so we tell the whole truth, and we experience the consequences of our choices. Students see and experience this freedom in our youth groups, and they are better prepared for the truth in their lives. Here's how that freedom might look.

1. Freedom means we are not afraid of untruth. When we walk in truth, we know we can trust it in all situations; we are not afraid to let it confront untruth. *All* ideas are welcome because we know truth will flourish and lead to Jesus. However, just because we are free to evaluate all ideas in light of truth doesn't mean we

When I approach high school principals with the idea of starting some type of Christian ministry (Bible Club, Fellowship of Christian Athletes, etc.) on their campuses, their responses often sound something like this: "I would love to, but if I let your group on campus, then I'd be forced to allow the Satanic Club on campus as well."

After citing the Equal Access Act to the principal in a gentle and respectful way, I never hesitate to say, "I'm not afraid of any Satanic Club on campus. I believe your students are smart enough to see through any type of satanic smoke screen."

The truth of Christ always leads to freedom, and we should never be afraid of telling the truth in youth ministry.

—Dave Ambrose

have to treat all ideas as equal. What it does mean is that we don't have to try to protect the truth by hiding it from those who want to analyze it. Freedom means we can show truth as it is and know that it will stand on its own.

2. Freedom means we tell the truth—the whole truth. We are free to tell even the not-so-nice parts: Jesus heals some, but doesn't heal all; the rain falls on the just and the unjust; Christianity causes great joy and great suffering; evil is real and vicious. We tell the *whole* truth, just like the Bible.

One part of the whole truth is that there are human elements in Scripture. The Bible is about people. People feel, cry, hurt, worry, doubt, panic, and fear, and we refuse to edit or doctor the text, to ignore the human aspect, to make it look good intellectually. For example, in John 21, Jesus appears to the disciples, and it's clear that the disciples are discouraged and depressed. It's great that Jesus came to earth; it's wonderful to know how much Jesus cared; but it's also important to know how difficult it was for the disciples to believe, *just as it is for us*.

The whole truth includes the rewards, too. Luke 24:13 describes two disciples who were walking along the road to Emmaus after the death of Jesus. Obviously, the two were depressed and lost as well. By the end of the story, though, their hearts were burning and their spirits were excited. There are times when the disciples hurt, and there are times when they delight in Christ's presence. The veracity of truth is that we can bounce from despair to happiness and back again.

3. Freedom means we experience the consequences of our choices. We may choose to jump from a building because the rush of the fall is what we want. The consequence is the crash at the bottom, and that may not be what we want. We can't have freedom of choice without consequence. Walking in truth has consequences, too. Life isn't lived in a philosophical vacuum, but in the trenches, and as we work there in truth, we make changes and are changed. What we do in this world matters.

Although warned, Peter betrayed Jesus, and he experienced the consequences. He felt alone angry with himself. He suffered with the memory of his betrayal for the rest of his life. However, Peter didn't choose despair; he chose to return to the Christ. This decision had consequences, too. One story about Peter's death indicates he was crucified upside down because he still felt the humiliation of his betrayal. Returning to Christ did not mean that Peter could eliminate the consequences of his betrayal; he continued to feel the pain of that moment until his death, but he did make another choice, and the consequences of that second choice reach beyond this world. We must be aware and remind our students that our decisions can change us in ways we aren't expecting.

Veracity shows that Truth creates honest discussion.

When our youth ministries have veracity, we allow kids to make wrong choices as well as correct ones, recognizing that adolescents are learning how to walk in the truth. Similarly, they are learning what untruth is, what it looks and feels like. By allowing them to learn and make mistakes, we recognize that living in the truth can show up in our mistakes as well as our successes.

We value honesty, even if the honesty exposes unbelief, weakness, or failure. Because we trust the truth, we are not worried or offended when ado-

I'm amazed at how arrogant I can be just because I'm an adult who communicates God's word to students. Unconsciously, I assume that truth is revealed only to "the teacher" and, by virtue of my age, I have a pipeline to the Holy Spirit that my students don't have. I've done the preparation—I am the authority! But instead of creating a life-changing encounter with truth, this attitude teaches students to passively await their spoon-feeding.

Ultimately, this can lead them to the dangerous conclusion that without someone to tell them what to believe, they can't move forward. To remedy this I need to see my preparation and experience as a means of facilitating a journey of shared discovery, not as a means of dispensing truth available only to me. If I really believe that truth flourishes in the exchange of ideas, perhaps I need to become more open to hearing the thoughts and insights of the teenagers I'm teaching.

The Holy Spirit has never discriminated on the basis of age—I shouldn't, either.

—*Marv Penner*

lescents are honest about their feelings or beliefs, and we accept their language or approach as long as it is honest.

If our ministries have veracity, we see the Christian life as a life of discovery, not as one lived through a dictated list of rules. Because the truth endures under the toughest scrutiny, people can think about it, challenge it, and discover it. In order to show students what it is like to live in the truth, we must teach them to think. If they don't think, they won't know the truth after they have left our groups.

This means creating a group in which students discuss, challenge, and question ideas, theirs and ours. Then our groups will have veracity, showing that the truth requires knowledge, not just blind acceptance. When we do this, the truth will make itself known. As Parker Palmer said, "I not only pursue truth, but truth pursues me. I not only grasp truth, but truth grasps me. I not only know truth, but truth knows me. Ultimately I do not master truth, but truth masters me" (*To Know as We Are Known*. Harper & Row, 1983. p. 59). Because we believe in the veracity of truth, because we trust the truth, we are willing to let truth run free.

Veracity shows that Truth can be tested.

Suppose you were thinking about buying a car. You might watch a video of the car and its features. Most likely you would sit in it, check the engineering, and analyze the safety components. However, it's the test drive that proves its veracity; it proves how well this car conforms to the truth about the make and model. Likewise, when our teenagers test drive what they learn about truth, they realize that it works in their lives, that they, too, can have lives of veracity.

Youth groups should be safe places of open dialogue, but they should also be places where students are encouraged to venture outside the artificial

> When I spoke on the AIDS crisis, we had more responses from students than we usually did. They wanted to help; they wanted to take part in a cause, in something bigger than themselves. Another time, when I addressed homosexuality, some students shared that they were struggling with their sexuality and needed someone to talk to. Each student thanked us for talking so openly about it.
>
> When we speak of the raw reality that comes with tough issues, we never know what kind of response we'll get, but we must be willing to take that risk. We must trust God to use us. We must speak the truth regardless of the consequences—that's our role as Christians.
>
> —*Megan Hutchinson*

environment of youth groups to enter the world. Some adults view church as a place removed from the real world, a place where only the right answers are discussed. Church, they believe, should be a place to hide from the world, not confront it. However, youth groups should not be country clubs or prep schools.

John cites a number of the disciples as saying, "This is a hard teaching. Who can accept it?" That is why youth group must provide a place where teenagers can test the truth. If they cannot test the truth in their lives, when

To me veracity means challenging parents who put a higher value on academics or sports than on their kids' spiritual growth. It means confronting students' lifestyle choices, knowing they may not be able to hear the truth right now. It means calling students to be radical disciples of Jesus, not calling them to be good citizens.

Veracity requires that we grow beyond our comfort levels, that we proclaim truth even when it's difficult. It means stating God's values, not our culture's or our church's values, even when it gets us in trouble. It's knowing that, in the long run, students will know we told them the Truth.

—*Tic Long*

they enter the world with truth, they might be overwhelmed. The difficulty of confronting the world with truth can lead many to despair. It has never been easy to follow Jesus, and our kids need to be aware of that. If we protect them and the truth from the outside, though, we will give them the impression that life with Jesus is easy. By allowing them to confront the world with truth in our youth groups, we give them the support and resources they need to manage the tension it creates.

Veracity shows that Truth is resilient.

Truth is resilient. It bounces back; it sticks; it lasts. Paul showed the resiliency of truth in his own life: "We are hard pressed on every side, but not crushed; perplexed, but not in despair; persecuted but not abandoned; struck down, but not destroyed" (2 Corinthians 4:8-9). The truth is resilient.

Because the goal of every youth ministry is resiliency, the question each youth worker must ask is, "What lasts?" This question has nothing to do with numbers, activities, or programs. It has to do with showing that truth endures. Veracity is one of our CORE realities because the most difficult

I believe developing kids' own resiliency should also be a goal. I work with junior highers, the most resilient creatures on earth, and I'm committed to nurturing that wonderful characteristic in each of them.

Recently I had to confront a group of boys for disrespecting the girls in our group. Their act was extreme, and so were the consequences. But as I called them to their responsibility to honor girls as God's property, not their own, I also assured them of God's promised forgiveness for confessed sin and his love for them—and my love for them. So while they were remorseful, because these young men are resilient, they were quickly back in the fold of the group and excited to start with a clean slate.

—*Heather Flies*

challenge of youth ministry is to explain the lastingness of the gospel. We want to walk in the truth to help students encounter truth in such a way that they don't forget it, they never leave it, and it remains an important part of their lives from this moment on.

This is not an easy task. Before we frustrate ourselves with impossible expectations, trying to do what can't be done, the Bible gives us some realistic parameters to consider when evaluating the veracity of our ministries. There are three concepts that can help ground us in reality even as we create youth groups that show truth is resilient.

1. The law of survivability. Jesus' parable about the farmer who sows his seeds (Matthew 13, Mark 4, Luke 8) gives us a glimpse of the amount of our work that will survive in the lives of teenagers. As a farmer scattered seed he was sowing, some fell along the path, and the birds came and ate it. Some fell on rocky places. It sprouted quickly because the soil was shallow, but when the sun came up, the plants withered because they had no roots. Other seed fell among thorns, which grew up and choked the plants. Still other seed fell on good soil, where it produced a crop 100, 60, or 30 times what was sown.

Jesus said a substantial amount of our efforts will not reap long-term results. First, some of what we do will be lost on those who hear it because it will be taken away from them quickly. Then a few will respond, but because they are not prepared for the truth, because their soil is not fertile, the truth will wither in their lives when it is exposed to the elements. Jesus goes on to say that fewer still will understand the truth enough for it to grow in

I used to measure the health of my youth ministry by the number of responses to my messages. I was always disappointed. Often I was tempted to manipulate my invitation to my kids to receive Christ because I desperately wanted to feel as if I were accomplishing something. Later I learned how unimportant all of those measurements are to the spiritual growth of my students. These days, on the rare occasion I feel compelled to measure anything, I'd much rather measure the number of times I presented the gospel and offered it to teenagers regardless of the responses. If we really believe the Holy Spirit is mysteriously working in the lives of our kids, it's our heart motives that are important, not the measured results.

—Dave Ambrose

their lives. Although those who really do understand may be few, the results in their lives will be multiplied.

2. The mystery of the harvest. In Matthew 13 Jesus follows the parable of the seeds with the parable of the weeds. He says the kingdom of God is like a man who sowed wheat seeds in his field, but that night his enemy sowed weeds among the wheat. When the wheat sprouted, so did the weeds, and it was difficult to tell

When I first started in youth ministry, I thought it was my responsibility to turn each of my students into a miniature Jesus. I would spend lots of time thinking through curriculum to be sure they'd be exposed to every major Christian doctrine so that by the time they left for college, they'd be able to understand and defend their faith without fail.

It wasn't until much later that I learned what a small role I played in the lives of "my" kids and how important parents, teachers, and other church leaders are to them.

I realize now that it's not my job to turn teenagers into mini Jesuses. My job is to wait around for Jesus to do his work in their lives, whenever and wherever he chooses. I've finally discovered that youth ministry is more about waiting and nurturing than about forcing students into my preconceived ideas of what spiritual students should look like.

—*Dave Ambrose*

the difference. If the farmer tried to pull out the weeds, he might also pull out the wheat. This parable gives us another truth that is hard to hear: *we* might not always be able to tell what is truth and what isn't until we can see its fruit. Often the people we think will survive don't, and those who we don't think will make it do. It's a mystery, Jesus tells us, and our job is to continue to be faithful, leaving the final harvest to him.

3. The presence of the weak and the strong. The Bible makes it clear that faith among the people of God varies. There are some who are strong in their faith and others who are weak. This means there are also multitudes of people who have faith somewhere in between strong and weak. In Romans 14, Paul discusses how to treat those who are weak, and weak faith is a serious issue in most youth groups because students can hide their own weak faith behind group experiences. A kid can worship for hours, attend concerts, and lead activities without really having a faith of his or her own. Many rely on a corporate faith, the faith of the group, and once they are away from the group, they don't have a faith that affects their lives. Because of this, it is important for those of us in youth ministry to address the needs of those who might have a weak faith, even if our students are enthusiastic during meetings. Then we can address the ways the faith professed in the group transfers to the decisions the students make at school and home.

Given the law of survivability, the mystery of the harvest, and the presence of the weak and the strong, it may seem impossible to ever know if our programs are resilient, if our walking in the truth has affected the lives of our kids. Yet if we stay faithful to the truth, it will take root in the lives of some and multiply. Although we might not know the effects our ministries have, we can work to ensure that when the truth does take root, it will be resilient.

To do this, to create resiliency even when we don't see the harvest, we must treat teenagers as students, realizing that maturity takes time and experience. *When we do this, we show the resiliency of truth: it is elastic and patient.*

The truth grows with the person it surrounds. As teenagers mature and experience more, they are capable of understanding more. As youth workers we must realize this and not expect them to be able to comprehend truth the way we do. Our experiences are bigger, and they need their own experiences for the truth to develop in their lives. If we try to make them fit a mature understanding of the truth, it will not adhere to their lives. We must give stu-

---

The first time I told my wife I loved her was on our second date, approximately 24 hours after our first date. I dated her for almost three years, and then on May 20, 1973, I married her.

When I told my wife I loved her more than 30 years ago, I really meant it, and when I told her this morning that I loved her, I really meant it. But what I meant when "I really meant it" more than 30 years ago is a lot different from what I meant when "I really meant it" this morning. How could it be otherwise? In 33 years we've shared a lot of life together—we've laughed, we've cried, we've raised a family, and we've shared a ministry.

Similarly, true spirituality requires an unchanging commitment to Jesus—but what "commitment to Jesus" looks like will constantly change. And that's how it should be. "Really committed to Jesus" for a 10-year-old should look quite different from "really committed to Jesus" for a 17-year-old.

—*Duffy Robbins*

Think about it—most difficult choices, I mean really difficult, are not between good and bad, but between good and good. Paul had tough decisions to make, too. He wanted to go to Macedonia because he deeply loved the church there. He had a "God-given opportunity," and although he struggled to find peace in his decision to go, he could not. It wasn't bad for Paul to go to Macedonia, and it wasn't bad for him to go elsewhere…the decision was between good and good, not good and bad.

In order to choose well between good and good, we have to dig deep into ourselves, into our desires, and into our motives. Does God want me to go to Pepperdine or UCLA? When it comes to tough choices between good and good, I wonder if God cares as much about what we choose as he cares about how we get there.

—*Dan Jessup*

dents the freedom to be young and trust the truth to stretch with them and to be patient with them as they mature.

I have to constantly trust in God that the seeds that have been planted, that I have watered and nurtured, will blossom. A number of years ago, a student in my youth group told me she was going into the ministry when she graduated from high school. The next year, she was planning to teach English in Mexico as a missionary. The following year, she decided to major in art; then she took off from school for a year; then she decided she did want to teach English, but here in the United States. Presently, she is still searching for a career path and goal, and I trust that the seeds of truth that were planted while she attended youth group are growing. Although she is not yet mature and the fruits have not yet developed, I can catch a whiff of the fragrance from the flowers of truth, so I continue to nurture and support her while she matures.

Veracity shows that Truth is attractive.

Many ministries have taken the vibrancy out of truth. Paul says that "through us spreads everywhere the fragrance of the knowledge of him. For we are to God the aroma of Christ among those who are being saved and those who are perishing" (2 Corinthians 2:14-15). When the young men and women in our youth groups begin to experience the truth of God, something begins to happen. As Paul says, people sense an aroma. They see the beauty and smell the fragrance of Christ. When people experience this, they want to be a part of it. When our youth groups have veracity, they will attract people we never expect. Once, a 16-year-old girl helped our youth group to have veracity, and

Evelyn M. McClusky was the mother of parachurch club ministry in the United States. In 1933 she gave birth to the Miracle Book Club in Portland, Oregon. She also published a series of books during the late '30s. At its peak the Miracle Book Club had a thousand chapters all over the United States. Evelyn attracted highly talented people, including Jim Rayburn and Al Metsker. Later, Jim Rayburn founded Young Life, and Al Metsker developed Kansas City Youth for Christ.

In 1998 I had an opportunity to visit Evelyn at her home in Atlanta, where she had lived for 60 years. She was 102 when I met her, and she was able to move around with her walker. Her mind was active and sharp. While there, I wanted to get a video clip of her talking to youth workers that I could use at the Youth Specialties convention. I spent an hour with her, but all I could get her to talk about was Jesus. She was amazing—working on her twentieth book and still talking with teenagers!

The 75-year-old woman who lived with her said Evelyn still introduces someone to Jesus each week. I asked for an example, and she told me about a UPS delivery the week before. Evelyn was watering her plants when the UPS man arrived to drop off a package. She engaged him in conversation for 15 minutes. He bowed his head as she prayed for him. When he looked up, he had tears in his eyes.

There was something about this spunky, engaging 102-year-old that I couldn't put my finger on. She was attractive; she had a fragrance, an aroma, about her (and not the "old-person smell"). Meeting Evelyn McClusky was one of the highlights of my year. She encouraged and inspired me by just being who she was.

—*Les Christie*

because of her willingness to test the truth, it attracted some unlikely characters.

During one meeting, this young woman raised her hand and interrupted my sermon on love. She said, "You are talking about love, but in three weeks, the county fair is coming, and most people in our town make fun of the carnies [carnival workers]. Since we're the church, and we believe in love, why don't we put on a dinner and welcome the carnies to town." Until that moment this young woman had not had much of a relationship with any of the adults in the church, but something began to flower. After the first successful carnie lunch (an all-you-can-eat affair for over 200 carnies), most of the adults in our church knew this young woman. They were attracted to her because of her veracity. Now, 13 years later, they still remember her, even though she has moved out of the area, has finished college, and owns her own business. This young woman not only showed the truth in her life, she helped our church to walk in the truth of Christ's love.

From the first carnie lunch until now, our church has never deliberately mentioned it is a church. We don't have fishes on our T-shirts or preach a sermon before lunch. This year, though, a tough young man without a shirt and with tattoos over most of his body approached me. His face was hard, and he sounded angry: "Are you in charge?"

I did think about telling him that Jill, the 13-year-old girl on the other side of the room, was. However, I mustered a "Yes."

"Is this a church?" He asked threateningly.

Again I was conflicted: "Uh, yes we are."

Then he pushed his face right next to mine and said, "I wanna tell you something, sir. If I lived here I'd go to this church." I don't know how he knew we were a church, but somehow he recognized the fragrance of Christ. The aroma of the gospel came through. Because of one young woman's veracity, years later others were attracted to the church, and ultimately, to Christ.

CORE Reality: Veracity

Veracity is at the heart of youth ministry. This appears in our youth groups when we show that the truth is freeing; it allows for honest discussions; it can be tested; it is resilient; and it is attractive. When our students are willing to let truth confront lies, challenge traditions, try out new ideas, grow and learn, and make their actions reflect the beauty of Christ. They want to express their faith to the rest of the church by conforming to the truth. This veracity is noticed by all who come in contact with them.

MANDATE: Youth ministry must expose students to the life-giving truth of Jesus Christ.

CHAPTER THREE

CORE REALITY

AUTHENTICITY

2 CORINTHIANS 6:3-13

2 THESSALONIANS 2:7-8

PHILIPPIANS 3:12-14

Mike's Story

I have issues about my past. You might have noticed that, in the introduction, I mentioned I was kicked out of Bible college…two of them. Although I flaunt my previous failures and brandish my expulsions as a badge of courage, an astute observer might realize I'm insecure about them as well. Only in the last few years of my life have I been able to wrestle my insecurities to the mat and accept who I am. Instead of seeing my flaws as blights on my record, I now see them as events God can use. Instead of hiding my weaknesses and hoping no one notices, I recognize that they are windows through which Jesus can be seen clearly. Because of my wild journey, I have a unique view of Jesus, which means that when I talk to students about my relationship with Jesus, it is different from anyone else.

It's taken me only 60 years to understand God's real love for authentic people and to realize what he wants from me is honesty, not piety. Maybe I do pastor the "slowest growing church in America." Maybe I am seminary-challenged. But for reasons I don't yet understand, God apparently needs a seminary-challenged, Bible-school-rejected, irregular disciple to reach those few seminary-challenged, Bible-school-rejected, irregular students that no one else can reach.

Am I still insecure? Yes. But at least now I know Jesus is not afraid of my insecurities and is more than willing to abide in my failures as well as my successes. He uses me best when I am authentic.

*A*uthentic means real, genuine. To be effective youth workers, we have to be real—not perfect, whole, together, complete, or competent—but real. We do not need to be afraid to show others we are imperfect. We should not fear exposing our messiness. Many people are worried that if students see their imperfections, they will reject Jesus. However, we must understand that when we deny our imperfections, we deny Jesus. Jesus knows who we are and understands our flaws and blemishes. He is not afraid to be associated with followers who are works in progress, striving for completion.

Authentic youth ministry doesn't condone sin or lower the standard of commitment; it exposes sin and raises standards by refusing to let those who falter run from their commitment to Christ. As disciples we are committed to following Jesus even though we are flawed. When we are authentic and honest about our failings, we move toward correcting them. We cannot hide our imperfection from teenagers. This doesn't mean, though, that we list all of our sins. It does mean that we should admit we don't have it all together.

If you are a parent working in a youth group your child attends, you know this. You can't hide. Your child knows the mistakes you've made,

---

One of the risks of ministry is transparency. Allowing students to see our hearts—the good, the bad, and the ugly—is an essential element of credibility.

On the other hand, should we really expect students to seek counsel from a youth worker whose life is in shambles? Logically, that would mean we should buy diets from fat people, hair growth products from bald people, and abstinence advice from Bill Clinton. As Ambrose, Bishop of Milan (A.D. 374-397), so vividly put it: "Who seeks for a spring in the mud? Who wants to drink from muddy water?...Who will think a man to be useful to another's cause whom he sees to be useless in his own life?...Am I to suppose that he is fit to give me advice who never takes it for himself?" Our students need to see that even though we are imperfect, we turn to God so that our blemishes can be healed—that we look at our own lives and take the plank from our own eyes.

—*Duffy Robbins*

---

knows you are far from perfect. You can't pretend. Although some of you might not wish it on your worst enemy, if we all had our own children in our youth groups, we would have to be authentic, which is good for our students and for us. Our students aren't looking for perfection; they are looking for authenticity.

In 1 Corinthians1:26-29, Paul clarifies what it means to be an authentic Christian:

> *Think of what you were when you were called. Not many of you were wise by human standards; not many were influential; not many were of noble birth. But God chose the foolish things of the world to shame the wise; God chose the weak things of the world to shame the strong, He chose the lowly things of this world and the despised things—and the things that are not—to nullify the things that are, so that no one may boast before him.*

No boasting. No pretending. No posing. We must come to youth group as we are: foolish, weak, and lowly. We don't have to confess all our sins to our students, and we shouldn't, but we do have to confess we are sinners even as we follow Jesus. Wow—we can all do that! Here are some ways we can start developing authenticity in our youth groups.

Share yourself.

In 1 Thessalonians 2:8 Paul tells one of the churches he worked with, "We loved you so much that we were delighted to share with you not only the gospel of God but our lives as well." Youth ministry is not about content alone; it's about content with context. When students get to know us, when they see us trying to live what we are teaching, when they see us trying to put the content of what we teach into the context of our lives, they are motivated to try it themselves.

This happened on one of my youth group's annual trips to Mexico. The other leaders and I were looking for adults who were experienced in construction and liked high school students. We found Bernie. He had construction experience and liked teenagers, but he made it very clear that he was not willing to counsel them, participate in the evening campfires, or attend morning Bible studies. Although he was a committed follower of Christ, he felt completely inadequate when it came to working with teenagers on a spiritual level. Bernie was shy and found it difficult to talk about God with teenagers—or so he thought. Because we liked him and knew he'd be a good addition to the work crew, we agreed that Bernie would not have to attend campfires or the morning Bible studies. The first night Bernie went to bed before campfire. The next day, students asked why he hadn't been to campfire and said they wanted to sit with him. He didn't go to campfire the second night, either, but he did sit just outside his tent and listen. By the third night, Bernie was sitting on the edge of the campfire and was shocked to hear what the group from his worksite said: "We worked with Bernie today, and he is so cool. He is really helpful and doesn't yell at us when we make a mistake. We loved working at his site." Bernie hadn't tried to be spiritual with the group, he hadn't tried to be holy—he simply was himself. When we got home, Bernie volunteered to help with the youth group and participated in the Mexico trip, including the evening campfires, for many more years. Bernie was authentic, and teenagers were attracted to him. They wanted to be taught by him because he was willing to share himself with them.

Teach the whole gospel...responsibly.

When people are authentic and share themselves, they tell the whole story of their lives, not just the clean parts. Scripture is filled with authentic people. We see the blemishes, warts, and brokenness of biblical characters: Sarai had her husband sleep with her servant; Jacob deceived his father and brother; Noah got drunk; Esther used her sex to buy freedom for some Israelites; Moses was a murderer; David was an adulterer and a murderer....We could go on and on. Major characters in the Bible are flawed and broken, yet somehow the magic and mystery of God's story shines through. Somehow God is able to communicate who he is by who we aren't. Somehow God reveals himself to and through those flawed characters, even when it is painful. Often, though, this part of the gospel is ignored: God does use us, even when we aren't perfect.

Many of us connect with Peter and smile when we think of him because he was so much like us. He was impulsive; so are we. He was hotheaded; so are we. It was Peter, the hotheaded, impulsive, inconsistent, weak, and frightened disciple who died following Jesus. Instead of his flaws causing us to reject him, they draw us to him. When we hear the whole story of Peter's fear, anger, betrayal, and death, we do not turn from Christ. In fact, when we see that Christ used even Peter, we realize Christ can use us. We also see that following Christ is tough. Peter struggled. He nearly drowned when he panicked while walking on water; he got into a couple of fights; he felt guilty for denying Jesus; and he was killed—not an easy life. Our students need to know that God can use them even though they are flawed and that his presence in their lives can make things dangerous, even scary, at times.

The whole story of Christ's life shows his struggles, too. When he was on the cross, Jesus cried, "My God, my God, why have you forsaken me?" (Matthew 27:46). This is not encouraging; it doesn't present a very positive picture of God, but it is part of the gospel. We see the struggle, the pain, and the despair of the crucifixion. If we were left with Jesus' forsaken statement, his death would have been bleak and difficult to understand. But Jesus wasn't done talking: "Father, into your hands I commit my spirit" (Luke 23:46). This is the whole story: the separation and the reunion, the suffering and the redemption. By showing it all, by not hiding the difficult parts, Christ impacted even his enemies—one of the Roman centurions exclaimed, "Surely he was the Son of God!" Authenticity, even when we are authentically questioning God, can be trusted to change the lives of those around us.

By teaching the whole gospel without editing the difficult parts, we are being responsible to the word of God and to our students. We also need to be responsible when we tell the whole story of our lives, share our struggles, and admit our failures. There is a difference between sharing and exhibiting, though: exhibitionists tell stories to draw attention to themselves; they are not concerned with the consequences. Authentic people are not exhibitionists, flaunting every sin they have ever committed. Students don't need to know the specifics; what they need to know is that we are not afraid to admit our imperfections.

> When we try to pretend that everything is perfect in our own lives, students see through it instantly. We fool ourselves when we think we can pull one over on students. They often know us better than we know ourselves!
> But we also need to be responsible when we admit our failings. If we use students to meet our emotional needs by sharing details of our lives in order to create some kind of shallow rapport or to elicit some kind of sympathetic response, we enter into a codependent relationship with them. Of course that is not healthy for anyone!
> —Marv Penner

When we are authentic, we tell the whole story—the bad and the good—responsibly. Teaching the whole gospel prepares students for a life with Jesus. We tell our stories to draw our students to him, but everything in the Bible points them to Jesus. Don't edit the Scriptures; don't tell students only the easy parts—tell them the whole story, so they can meet the whole Jesus. It doesn't take a lot for people to be drawn to truth—just authenticity and responsibility.

Ask for help.

If, as authentic people, we are able to admit our failings and teach the whole gospel, then we must also be able to ask for help. Being authentic doesn't mean being skilled, strong, and always capable. Authentic means we acknowledge that we don't always know what to do. This isn't always easy for us because many teenagers, and even their parents, believe youth workers have all the answers. When people come to us for help and advice, we often don't like to admit that we can't help or don't know what advice to give. Sometimes this is because we like to have our egos boosted; other times it is because we don't want to let down one of our students. Whatever their reasons for doing so, most youth workers who decide to counsel others get involved with much more than they can handle and give bad advice. This is why we recommend that youth workers don't become counselors: most of us aren't trained to be counselors.

> Many youth workers arrogantly believe they have all of the answers when it comes to their ministries. Oddly, they imply that they don't even need God to show up because their programs run like well-oiled machines. They talk about how big their ministries are and how many students are making decisions to receive Christ. I'm weary of talking to youth workers who believe they know what needs to be done in youth ministry—because they don't. Often they just don't want to ask for help, afraid that would look bad. Worse, some think they don't *need* help.
>
> We need more youth workers who admit they don't have a clue. We need youth workers who have more questions than answers. We need youth workers who are learning what it means to depend upon God to lead them every day in their ministries! Maybe then we'll allow room for our students to feel safe enough to admit they don't have it all together, either. Maybe then we'll allow enough room for God to do what he really wants to do in and through our ministries.
>
> —*Dave Ambrose*

Our job is to be authentic, which means to care for them, listen to them, affirm them, and refer them—not fix them. There is nothing wrong with youth workers saying, "I don't know. I have no clue," because we can also say, "I'll get back to you. Let me see if I can find someone who can help you." Of course, the most reliable and powerful resource we have is God, and when the issues become tangled and involve families, it's time to fall back on what the church has always done…pray.

I know of one youth worker who was able to ask for help, and he discovered that he could get help from his own students. Dan worked in an urban church and saw the devastation of the students in these areas. Moved by the plight of urban youth, he and his wife became foster parents for older teenagers who needed a solid home. One Wednesday afternoon, a few hours

When I was a youth pastor in Berkeley, California, I was about to teach a lesson on God's faithfulness. Suddenly, I realized I wasn't feeling God's faithfulness at all. Instead of going ahead with my preplanned talk, I decided to take a huge risk and get real.

I looked down, too embarrassed to make eye contact with my students, and began my confession: "I'm about to teach this lesson on God's faithfulness, and I need to tell you something. I've had some big disappointments lately, and I haven't been feeling God's faithfulness at all. So I'm having a hard time trying to teach you about it." After a few more sentences describing my predicament, I ended about as feebly as I began: "I guess what I need is for you guys to pray for me." A hush fell across the room. I thought everyone had left. Instead, to my amazement, I looked up to find the eyes of every student riveted on me. (I believe it is the only time in my youth ministry career that this ever happened.) Gently, the students broke the silence and offered to pray for me. And an amazing thing happened—I stepped off my spiritual pedestal, and we all went to Jesus together that day.

God managed to weave together an incredible Sunday school lesson from the ashes of my confession. And I learned an invaluable truth: as youth workers we don't need to "be Jesus." We just need to be ourselves. Jesus speaks for himself.

—*Laurie Polich*

before the evening activity and Bible study, Dan's wife called him at church. Their foster son had physically attacked her. She was bruised and traumatized. Immediately he went home to calm his wife and deal with their foster son. After a difficult and exhausting few hours, Dan came to the junior high meeting drained and incapable of teaching. Standing before the students, he said, "Hey, folks, I'm pretty wiped out tonight. Our foster son and wife got into a fracas, and my wife is pretty shaken, and so am I. So I just don't have anything..." Before he could finish, the junior high students stood up, surrounded him, and began to pray. They decided to share the responsibilities for the Bible study that evening so that Dan could go home and be with his wife.

Dan was willing to admit life wasn't going well—that he couldn't do it and needed help. Because of this, his students grew, took on new challenges, and offered help to the person who had spent his life helping his students. Authenticity involves the humility and courage to show students where they can get help, to show them the help Christ can provide. If we are authentic, we can say, "I don't have all the answers, and I don't really know why this works, but I believe Jesus can somehow satisfy what you are looking for. In some mysterious way Jesus' presence can be enough." When teenagers see us asking for help, using our resources, leaning on others, and praying, they will learn that they, too, can pray and ask for help when they need it.

Strive for righteousness.

People who are authentic need help because they are not perfect. Authentic youth workers are not godly, but they want to be, so they work toward being godly. In Philippians 3:12-14, Paul explains this:

> *Not that I have already obtained all this, or have already been make perfect, but I press on to take hold of that for which Christ Jesus took hold of me. Brothers, I do not consider myself yet to have taken hold of it. But one thing I do: Forgetting what is behind and straining toward what is ahead, I press on toward the goal to win the prize for which God has called me heavenward in Christ Jesus.*

Paul nails it. He is authentic. He has not attained perfection, has not finished the battle, yet he continues to "press" and "strain" toward God—he strives for righteousness. We, too, are working at it; we're making every effort to hang on to Jesus, and when we do this in our youth groups, we are creat-

---

I understand that authenticity means I am to be the best I can, pressing on in my faith—but I have a hard time with the word *striving*. It implies that I am the one responsible for the spiritual change and growth that happens in me. Over 600 times in the Bible, God or Jesus says, "Come to me." I think that God does require us to come to him, but he is the one that does the work.

—Helen Musick

---

ing authenticity. Our students will recognize this.

What our students also will recognize is that even if we're not hanging on very well, Jesus is hanging on to us. When we are authentic and students see that even though we sometimes fail, we continue to strive to improve our relationship with Jesus, they will understand that it is not by our strength we can do it, but by God's. As youth workers, we should not deny our failures. Rather we should admit our failures and learn from them so that we may strive for righteousness and help our students strive for righteousness, too. Then we will be acting authentically.

Trust your uniqueness.

If a shirt is an authentic Polo shirt, there is a little polo rider somewhere on the shirt, which means, of course, that this "authentic" polo shirt is exactly like thousands of other "authentic" polo shirts. Fortunately, authentic means something different in youth ministry. When we strive to be righteous, we

> I remember the day I was no longer "cool." I'd been doing youth ministry for about eight years and was now old enough—28—to not wear the latest fads. Still I tried my hardest to look like I wasn't that far off track. I was walking with a group of middle school students when I noticed them laughing at something…ME! I was wearing orange socks—you know, to match my orange shirt. Little did I know that white socks were "in," regardless of shirt color. I must admit I felt a little insecure for a moment. Then I remembered I was an adult—I could handle this! Being effective with students means we have a sense of our self apart from their opinions. Sure we want to be able to relate, but students don't need another student to care for them; they need adults who are secure enough to get beyond their own insecurities. We all had a great laugh (but I did go home and throw out all my colored socks)!
>
> —Helen Musick

use the unique gifts God has given us, so being authentic in youth ministry means the unique way each one of us does ministry—the unique way *you* do ministry. When we rely on our individuality and use our unique talents, God will work powerfully through us.

I saw this happen when my wife and I handed over the ministry we had been leading to new leaders. For years Karla and I had volunteered as leaders in a very small town in Northern California. With a couple of exceptions, we ran our youth group like most youth groups in America: weekly meetings, more serious Bible studies, and camps. We had about 10 percent of the high school students attending our program, and those teenagers were mostly the leaders in the school, the athletes, and the popular students. After 10 years of leading this group, Karla and I decided to step down, and a young couple took over. Gary had attended youth group when he was in high school, and he and his wife were excited about reaching students.

After a few weeks of training, it became clear that Gary couldn't run this group the way it was *supposed* to be run. He didn't sing or play the guitar, and his skits were terrible. He wasn't very good at speaking, either. Meetings were a disaster, and attendance dwindled. My wife and I were concerned, but Gary wasn't. One day he announced that the group wasn't going

There are students God wants to reach through you just as you are (as frightening as that might be). I'm a loud, emotional, outgoing, and, at times, unpredictable guy. I have never been good at connecting with quiet, reflective students; I scare them. My years in youth ministry have taught me that I better include people very unlike me on my ministry team, so students unlike me can be ministered to as well. If you think you don't fit with the rest of the leaders, that you are really different from others working with students at your church—that's great! You're very likely a gift from God to your leadership team—a team that now more resembles the body of Christ.

—*Tic Long*

to have regular meetings anymore, and he began an early-morning breakfast meeting at a local restaurant, just to hang out with students. The more serious Bible study became a Monday Bible study with pool and other table games, and he stopped taking the group to camps. Instead Gary took the group to Mexico or the inner city to work with the poor. He also developed a work program for youth at the high school who were in trouble or on probation. He connected with a number of social service organizations such as Habitat for Humanity. And—get this—he would take the students to garage sales every weekend.

At first Karla and I were appalled. The group's parent organization told Gary he couldn't use the official name anymore. Parents of the popular students complained about their children losing interest. When Karla and I investigated, though, we discovered that Gary was now actively involved in the lives of 150 students at the high school. The morning breakfasts had 20 to 40 students, and another 20 attended the Monday-night event. On weekends, between 30 and 50 teenagers would go to garage sales, on one-day mystery trips, or on other outings with them. Most of the students Gary ministered to were those on the fringe: ethnic minorities, youth at risk, troubled teens, and students who had fallen through the cracks. Gary and his wife had created their own ministry, uniquely based on their many skills and gifts. The impact of their ministry was at least as powerful (if not more) as the impact of the traditional ministry my wife and I had for years; it is just that the impact was different, unique.

God works most powerfully when we acknowledge the individual talents he has given us. When we begin to trust these unique gifts, our youth ministries will become authentic.

Individualize relationships.

Just as we should recognize and trust our own unique qualities, we should recognize and trust the unique qualities of others. Authenticity can't be franchised; it doesn't have a formula; there is no one way authenticity looks. When we treat others authentically, we take each person as a unique individual. What works most effectively in a highly franchised, technological society is a nonfranchised, nontechnological relationship. What works in a highly impersonal culture is a highly personalized response. By taking into account each student's past, present, and personality, we can build a relationship with that individual based on who we are and who that young person is—we build authentic relationships.

> The most valuable paintings are originals, not copies of originals. So I encourage my students to be themselves, not to try to copy someone else. When I'm with them, I encourage my students to be who they are in real life, not just "youth group life"—and we should treat them as the people they are in real life.
>
> —Les Christie

Building individualized relationships takes time. It takes energy. To get to know someone as an individual, to learn his or her quirks, needs, and fears, we must spend time with that person and listen to what that person says and asks. Instead of giving a programmed response to what we think a student might be saying, we should try to discover the question or need a student has, which might be masked by what that student says or does. In order to do this, in order to respond to the individual, we have to understand that person's unique qualities.

One youth group exemplified this type of authenticity when a high school girl confessed to them that she was pregnant. Because she decided to have the baby rather than get an abortion, the father had left her. Often this teen's youth worker had made clear that having sex before marriage was not what God intended, and she also made it clear that she believed abortion was wrong. Faced with a young girl in her youth group who obviously had sex before marriage but had decided not to have an abortion despite the advice of her boyfriend and family, the youth worker met with others from the youth group.

Deciding to address her as an individual, not simply as a pregnant girl, they nominated a small group of girls to take the place of the father. They attended birthing classes together and agreed to take shifts during the delivery. Of course many in the church criticized the youth worker for condoning immoral behavior. The youth worker, however, believed the opposite. She wasn't condoning sex outside of marriage; she was treating this girl as an authentic person and being authentic herself. This youth worker showed this young, scared, pregnant girl what church really is—a place were we are safe, where sinners can be redeemed. The girl already knew she had done something wrong, and she didn't need to be reminded by others; she was experiencing the consequences of that. What she needed was someone to respond to her, individually, and find the authentic way to redeem what had gone wrong. And her youth group did.

When we treat people as individuals, we are not only treating them as authentic people and being authentic ourselves, we are showing that Christ is authentic. Christ reaches out to us as individuals, and he meets our individual needs. Each one of us has an individual relationship with Christ, and our redemption is a response to our individuality. If we are truly authentic, we will also recognize the authenticity of others, and they will see the authenticity of Christ.

CORE Reality: Authenticity

We put no stumbling block in anyone's path, so that our ministry will not be discredited. Rather, as servants of God we commend ourselves in every way; in great endurance; in troubles, hardships, and distresses; in beatings, imprisonments and riots; in hard work, sleepless nights and hunger; in purity, understanding, patience and kindness; in the Holy Spirit and in sincere love; in truthful speech and in the power of God; with weapons of righteousness in the right hand and in the left; through glory and dishonor, bad report and good report; genuine, yet regarded as impostors; known, yet regarded as unknown; dying, and yet we live on; beaten, and yet not killed; sorrowful, yet always rejoicing; poor, yet making many rich; having nothing, and yet possessing everything.

(2 Corinthians 6:3-10)

This is Paul's defense of his ministry. People criticized Paul and his friends for the way he taught about God. However, Paul makes it clear that he didn't want to disillusion those to whom they ministered, he didn't want to cause them to question Jesus Christ, so Paul and those with him showed themselves at their best *and* at their worst: when they were distressed *and* when they were patient; when they were in prison *and* when they were ministering at people's houses; when they were strong *and* when they were weak; when their lives were good *and* when they were bad. What Paul emphasizes is that they were authentic. They hid nothing. And rather than their imperfections driving people away from Christ, they drew people to him.

MANDATE: Authentic youth workers will draw teenagers to Jesus Christ.

CHAPTER FOUR

CORE REALITY

AUDACITY

MATTHEW 10:34

JOHN 2:13-21

EPHESIANS 6:19

2 TIMOTHY 1:7-8

Mike's Story

In most churches, summer means Vacation Bible School. Magnolia Baptist Church was no different. For decades at this church, VBS was the summer program for kindergarten through sixth-grade students. In my first summer of youth ministry at Magnolia Baptist Church, I naively asked, "Why don't you have a summer program for junior high kids?" The staff looked at me like I was crazy and listed the reasons:

1. Junior high students would rather be at the beach, which was only a few miles away.
2. VBS sounds like it's for elementary students, and junior high students would be embarrassed to participate.
3. Junior high students couldn't get transportation to and from the church.
4. Most obviously, junior high students are too wild.

Audaciously, I decided to have a junior high VBS anyway, much to the displeasure of the ministry staff. During our VBS, the boys made boogie boards for the surf and the girls made peasant dresses, which were groovy in those days. We also created a drama, played games, and studied the Bible. Sixty kids attended, and on the final night the junior high drama was the hit of the evening.

I learned a good lesson that summer: youth ministry requires audacity. Because I didn't know any better, the summer program was better. My ignorance of the tradition allowed me to stumble through new territory, and to the surprise of the staff, Jesus was there.

Much of our ministry is spent cutting our way through the objections, traditions, and fears of those around us. Jesus cut through the objections, traditions, and fears of the synagogue staff members—he was audacious. His life is our example, and that's good enough for me.

Audacity means bold, daring, and fearless. We don't use the word *audacity* in the context of spirituality very often, though, because it doesn't sound very spiritual. If, however, we glance through Scripture, it is clear that audacity is at the heart of Jesus' ministry. Thus it should be at the heart of youth ministry. The incarnation was the most audacious decision God could have made, boldly entering this world in flesh, only to be crucified. The gospel rests on the audacity of a God who humiliated himself to rescue us. So, of course, those of us who follow Christ should be known for the same audacity that Jesus possessed.

After Christ's death and resurrection, as churches were established, Paul reminded congregations that they must be bold in order to live the Christian life. In fact, he tells Timothy to "fan into flame" the gift of God because

> I think one reason the gospel has lost some of its compelling nature for this generation is because we have neutered its audacity. We have reduced its message to behavioral modification rather than spiritual transformation. Control has superceded passion, and we sound more like schoolmarms than prophets and priests; meanwhile the best story ever has become just another list of nice platitudes. Audacity marks many of the great movies and novels we love to quote, and it ought to mark our telling and our living of the gospel today.
>
> —*Charley Scandlyn*

"God did not give us a spirit of timidity" (2 Timothy 1:6-7). Churches, Christians, and youth groups should not be known for being demure; they should be on fire, "fanning into flames" the power of the gospel. Again in Ephesians 6:19, Paul speaks of the need for disciples to be bold; he tells them to pray that he will "fearlessly make known the mystery of the gospel." Already he had been arrested, and he was ready to be arrested again!

The disciples learned their audacity from Christ. At 12 years old, Jesus boldly walked into the temple and discussed religion with the rabbis. Throughout his life he audaciously confronted church and political leaders. He crashed into the temple and overturned the money changers' tables. He healed on the Sabbath. He marched his disciples through a cornfield on the Sabbath. He did not reprimand those who destroyed the roof of someone else's house. He alienated his hometown. He met with and taught tax collectors, prostitutes, and zealots. And he destroyed the pig-farming business in one city. Wow! This was a man who did what others never expected. Jesus was bold, daring, and fearless—he was audacious.

Jesus' audacity made him enemies, threatened the religious power structure, alienated those outside the church, and even made his own people want to kill him. Because he was audacious, he gave health to the sick, sight to the blind, hope to the hopeless, power to the powerless, and life to the lifeless. He also destroyed powerful kingdoms, altered history, conquered death, and made it possible for us to become the children of God, heirs with Christ, God's own people. Jesus, the wild, untamed, dangerous, reckless, threatening, risky, irresponsible, daring, rash savior of the world "made himself nothing, taking the very nature of a servant, being made in human likeness... humbled himself and became obedient to death, even death on a cross!" (Philippians 2:7-8).

Over the last 2,000 years or so, Christianity became tame, docile, and timid. Churches accepted the status quo in politics, art, and society. In short they became comfortable with institutionalism. If we as youth workers want a ministry that follows Christ's, we need to challenge our culture when it is destructive; we need to expose the greed of the money changers; and we need to confront the church when it is complacent. An audacious youth ministry looks like an explosion. It is not clean; it is messy, and we make mistakes. Because of this, our ministries often will be misunderstood, but it is in the midst of this mess that the most creative ministry can be done. All it takes is a bit of courage and a willingness to follow Christ. Here are some of examples of what can happen when we have audacity.

In his book *The Empty Church: The Suicide of Liberal Christianity,* Thomas Reeves comments that we have introduced our teenagers not to the God of Israel, mighty in both his love and his wrath, but rather to a God who is "wholly and merely nice." Our big challenge to teenagers has simply been to call them to a life that is nice and harmless since our father in heaven is nice and harmless—kind of one part Jesus, two parts Oprah, and five parts Mr. Rogers.

In our youth ministries we need to return to our mandate of making wild-eyed and dangerous disciples of Jesus. Youth ministry is more than finding the lost sheep; it's turning lost sheep into young lions.

—*Duffy Robbins*

There is an explosion of the Holy Spirit.

The audacity of the gospel is that, for us to grow as Christians, we have to move from our places of comfort to places of discomfort. Discomfort is a symptom of the presence of the Holy Spirit; it is the call of God to move. The book of Acts describes what happens when the Holy Spirit shows up—

there's an explosion with "a violent wind" and "tongues of fire" (Acts 2:2-3). The Holy Spirit brings a power that destroys boundaries, leading people into the unknown. As Peter says in Acts 2, this spirit brings people visions and dreams; it can even break the boundaries of death. Throughout the rest of Acts, we see what can happen to people who are stirred by the Holy Spirit: arrest (chapters 4 and 5), death (chapters 6 and 7), and persecution

So what happens when my ministry is not "exploding"? What do I do when things seem to be shrinking more than they are growing? How do we understand the movement of the Holy Spirit when common Christian culture says that when we're "blessed," our ministries grow 10 to 20 percent a year? Let me offer three basic thoughts:
1. God tends to find ways to make sure he gets the credit and no one else. In Judges 7 we read that Gideon's army dropped from 30,000 to 300 men, and it pleased the Lord. If Gideon's earthly boss had been receiving hourly reports on Gideon's leadership, Gideon may have been unemployed before the battle ever began.
2. In the days following the crucifixion, just about everyone who had been following Jesus took off—even some of his closest buddies abandoned him. A movement that people believed would overthrow the evil Roman Empire seemed to do nothing but get a few people stoned to death and their leader flogged and crucified. For all practical purposes, this movement was a miserable failure. And yet apparent failure was just the beginning of the greatest success of all time.
3. Pruning seems to be part of the ministry of the Spirit, which, to the realistic and pragmatic eye, may look more like failure than success. Read John 15; things get cut and removed all the time.
There are seasons to life, seasons to ministry, and seasons to our spiritual growth, so before we assess the "success or failure" of a ministry, we must determine which season that ministry is in.

—Dan Jessup

(chapter 8). This doesn't stop the explosion, though. Filled by the Holy Spirit, the apostles broke boundaries and moved into the unknown. They were audacious, and others, even those in the religious community, were troubled at what looked like an uncontrollable explosion—the church kept growing! The authorities tried to contain it, but even by killing apostles, they couldn't stop it.

Mark Dowds is living proof that the explosion of Holy Spirit in youth ministry will be resisted, even by the church. By allowing the spirit to move him from comfort to discomfort, he began an audacious youth ministry that affected hundreds. Mark had a passion to reach unchurched teenagers in

I have a friend in Chicago who has started "spoken word" sessions at his youth group. He says the results have been amazing. Students are creating poems, talks, and raps on different subjects. Sometimes it gets pretty scary (you don't know what a young person might share), and the audacity of students to tell the truth about their lives always generates a lot of interesting—often explosive—discussion. They can be audacious because they sense freedom and trust each other. And the truth flourishes. (Try it one night at your youth group! You can find out information about the spoken word craze by searching for "spoken word, poetry" on the Internet.)

—*Fred Lynch*

Belfast, Northern Ireland, and began an outreach ministry in the suburban town of Bangor. He rented the most popular nightclub—the Boom-Boom Room—and started what could best be described as a dance/techno church service on Sunday nights. It was a huge success: hundreds of teenagers came and heard about Jesus. The owner of the club dropped by one Sunday night, and after seeing the crowds, pulled Mark and the club manager aside. "Are we charging him to use the club?" he asked the manager. The manager responded, "Of course!" The owner, who was not a Christian, said, "I've never seen anything like this in all my life: your DJs are better than the ones we find, and the kids are having fun without damaging the place or harming each other; there's something unique here that I can't figure out. Whatever it is, you'll never be charged to use this place again." The Holy Spirit was working, exploding boundaries and taking people into the unknown.

And the churches freaked. A collective of churches in the area denounced the ministry, saying publicly that Mark was a heretic and opposed to the church. They were so afraid of the changes that they persecuted Mark, spreading lies to try to stop him. Eventually, under great pressure, Mark decided he had to close the ministry. The authorities stopped him because he had the audacity to try something different; the church was afraid of the uncontrollable explosion. He had gone too far for the institution. Mark believed in an audacious gospel, an audacious savior, an audacious Holy Spirit.

There are messy mistakes.

Most youth workers read books, listen to audio tapes and CDs, watch DVDs, and attend seminars so they can learn how to do their jobs with fewer mistakes. But the truth is that often mistakes are the fruit of audacious ministry; they are a result of the explosion. Sometimes it is in our mistakes, in our messiness, that the best ministry is done. Through trial and error, by experimenting, we learn how to do youth ministry the best we can with the students we've been given.

This is exactly what the followers of Jesus did. First they tried to keep the children away from Jesus, but Jesus told them that was wrong, so they brought the children to him. Then they kept the blind and sick away from Jesus, but they realized quickly that wouldn't work, so they searched for the

> I had just been hired as a part-time youth worker in a Garden Grove, California, church where the youth room was painted a dingy, hospital-white color. The youth group, based on my suggestion, decided to paint the room. So I rounded up cans of donated paint and met with the kids at 7 a.m. the next Saturday. We couldn't agree on a color, so we compromised and painted each wall a different color: one white, one black, one red, and the last blue. We cleaned up and went out to breakfast. Mission accomplished.
>
> What I did not know was that another group met in that room while the youth group was in the first worship service: the senior citizens.
>
> During the first worship service, I was beaming. I felt proud of the work our teenagers had done—until the senior pastor slid into the chair next to me and told me how upset the senior citizens were. He told me I could kiss my job goodbye, that he couldn't save me, that I was dead meat. I had made a big, messy mistake.
>
> Immediately, I went to the room, and before the senior citizens could say anything, I asked if they had noticed the room had been painted. They had. I then told them how excited I was to work in a church where high schoolers were so spiritual: the wall on the left was blue to symbolize heaven; the wall on the right was red to symbolize the blood of Christ; the wall behind them was black, which stood for sin, and they sat facing away from that wall; and the wall at the front of the room, the wall they faced, was white, which stood for purity. What could the senior citizens say?
>
> Then I grabbed the high schoolers to tell them what they should say if anyone ever asked why we selected those colors. For 15 years God used my messy mistake to remind people of Jesus.
>
> —Les Christie

blind and sick to heal. Most of the time Jesus' followers were just confused because they didn't know what he would do next. Refreshing, isn't it? In this culture of palm pilots and cell phones, meetings and lunches, programs and classes, it is comforting to know that not everything can be planned and prepared, that mistakes happen, and that God can use those, too.

Disciples often end up not knowing what to do, and Jesus answers "Trust your I don't know." Trust your lack of experience, your lack of clarity.

Out of your ignorance will come a knowledge you didn't know possible. Out of your blindness will come a seeing you didn't know you could have. Don't be afraid to try what has never been tried before or do what hasn't been done before.

In fact, a healthy relationship with Jesus always takes us where we've never been and shatters our stereotypes and biases. Stick with Jesus, seek him first, and "We've always done it this way" will be changed to "We've never done it this way." "This will never work" will be change to "It worked!" "Oh, God could never use that" will become "Wow! Look what God used."

There is creativity.

Because audacious youth ministry is messy, it also must be creative so we can make something out of the mess. When traditional ministry doesn't work, when someone has the audacity to challenge it, there must be a ministry to go in its place. Developing this requires us to be creative, to look at what we have and use it in new ways, to approach teenagers differently. When Jesus called to the disciples and told them to fish on the other side of the boat, he called them to do something different (John 21). The typical response would probably be, "If we couldn't catch fish here, why would changing sides be any different?" But it was. Even small changes, slight adjustments to the way we see people and situations, can make enormous differences. When we look at our situations differently, when we see new ways to do ministry, when we are creative, the possibilities are amazing.

Perhaps you have seen situations like the following where some really audacious youth ministry could have been done but wasn't. At a church with a substantial parking lot, a group of skaters began using the handicapped ramp and railings at the back of the lot for practice. Often the skaters would fly across the parking lot, barely missing people's vehicles, and sometimes they would skate through the office walkways on their way to school. As soon as the church janitor noticed, he asked the church board to buy signs and to place obstacles in the area so no one could skate there. Soon signs were posted: "No skaters allowed on church grounds" and "Skateboarding not allowed."

If this situation had been addressed creatively, a new ministry could have developed. Of course the problems of insurance, destruction of property,

I'm fortunate to be a part of a church that understands creativity and audacity go hand in hand. In my youth group, we listen to songs from the secular music chart's top 40 list and watch video clips from recent movies. We use the songs and video clips to connect the kids to topics that we are investigating, studying, or introducing.

Some people complain about this approach. "Isn't church supposed to be the place where we honor God?" they ask. Yes! And honoring God means communicating truth in a way that those who don't yet understand or know him will "get" truth. This means that often we have to be a bit edgy and creative...even audacious.

Jesus did this all the time: hanging with the outcasts, telling stories most people didn't understand, and turning the religious establishment upside down. Offending someone may not be an indication of doing something "wrong" but an indication that we have sided with Jesus.

—*Helen Musick*

and danger to nonskaters have to be addressed, but rather than posting prohibitive signs, which is the typical reaction, the church could have looked at it another way. Wouldn't it have been audacious if the church board had decided to allocate the funds that they used to prohibit the skaters toward building a permanent skate ramp in the back corner of the parking lot with signs that read, "Skaters Welcome"? This would've cost a substantial amount of money, and insurance costs would've risen, but it would have shown Jesus to a completely new group of students and solved the other problems: with a designated ramp and skate area, skaters would be less likely to fly through the rest of the parking lot and church. The church could even build a skateboard holder at the front of the sanctuary so the skaters could come to church on Sunday. Perhaps the youth worker could hang fliers around the church advertising a day trip to a skate park a few hours drive away. There are hundreds of other possible creative solutions, some costing more than others and most taking more time than posting signs. However, the effort of creating a new ministry, of reaching a new group of teenagers, is well worth it: audacious, creative, and amazing!

Not only can we find creative and audacious ways to bring our ministries to new students, but we can also find new ways of bringing students to our ministries. Here's an update of a biblical story in which a person is creatively brought to Christ. Eric has been suffering from a serious disease, and recently, doctors have stated they think they have found a cure. A new miracle drug had been released in small amounts to only one hospital in the country so it can be tested on a limited basis. People suffering from the disease were cautioned that it would take years before the enough of the drug could be produced for and distributed to the general public. Eric's youth group and church had been praying for a cure for years, and they believed this was it.

When the youth group heard about the new miracle drug, they knew that they needed to get Eric to the doctors who could cure him. His local doctors said Eric didn't have much time, certainly not enough time to wait for the drug to be tested. Even though the test hospital was located hundreds of miles away, the youth group drove Eric to the hospital. When they arrived, it was impossible to get into the building. However, this was an audacious youth group. They quickly devised a creative way to get into the building. Climbing onto the roof, they forced open a skylight so they could drop their friend through the ceiling into the hospital. It took only a few minutes for security to be alerted; the youth group members were arrested and charged with numerous offenses. However, the doctors in the hospital realized the youth group's passion for Eric and Eric's desire to live. They had compassion and treated him. Of course the church fired the youth worker, reprimanded the kids, and immediately created new policies to guard against such offenses happening again, but Eric was alive. Because of their creativity and audacity, they had been able to get Eric to the only people who could save him.

In Mark 2 and Luke 5, this is exactly what the four friends did for the paralyzed man, and Jesus had compassion on them. He saw past the destruction of property and into their passion for life. We, of course, are not suggesting youth workers find ways to break laws; however, we are suggesting that the law shouldn't limit your passion for introducing kids to Christ. Jesus was continually accused of being a lawbreaker because he was more interested in healing people than in lifeless laws.

If we, too, are concerned with Christ's work, we will be more concerned about people than about the dictates of a church board, a city, or a government. When we fall back on the laws, situations are solved in the same old ways, and often that doesn't yield the results we want. Faced with situations that seem fruitless, we can be creative, find new ways to do ministry, search for different answers to the same old problems. This, to others, is audacity.

There is misunderstanding.

Often people in authority misunderstand audacious ministry. Because it is different and new, they believe it is wrong. The Pharisees were like this; because they misunderstood Jesus' creative ministry, they were continually

> Beware! Audacity can quickly become arrogance—or at least others might see it as arrogance. Audacious ministry walks a fine line. When I boldly paint outside the lines and bypass tradition for the sake of what I believe will create a more effective ministry, I can easily alienate people who are less resilient to change than I am. I need to remember that ministry always happens in the context of community. A "big picture" perspective reminds me that Christ's law of love supercedes my need to do it my way. My tendency has been to run ahead whether people are with me or not. I'm learning, though, that I can stay balanced when I look around for new and perhaps audacious ideas while listening carefully to the wisdom and insight of others in my ministry.
> —*Marv Penner*

angry with him for his audacity. When Jesus broke the Sabbath by healing a crippled woman (Luke 13:10-17), they understood that he was breaking the law. What they did not understand, though, is that Jesus was enabling this woman to fulfill the law, to rest on the Sabbath. They believed healing was work, but Jesus points out this misunderstanding. By comparing his actions to relieving an ox of its yolk, he teaches that healing this woman frees her to worship God.

We, too, are often misunderstood when our ministries are audacious. If we use popular music, many say we are "secularizing" the youth group. Similarly, if we indicate a "C" on a report card is not the end of the world, many say we teach our kids weak values. In fact, much of the misunderstanding that occurs is not only from church leaders, but also from parents.

Ask youth workers what the number-one problem is for students today, and most will say "stress." teenagers are stressed out because they are too busy, too scheduled, too pressured by…the world…er…no…by the devil…um…not really…by their parents… Sadly, yes, their parents. Increasingly, parents put pressure on their children to attend pre-SAT classes, dance classes, hockey camps, football camps, or cheerleading camps. Youth workers are expected to acquiesce to the crowded schedules of the students in the youth group.

Once, a senior pastor misunderstood me even when the message was

clear to his students. During the first night's message at a week-long conference in Florida, I mentioned that my wife was not a typical youth pastor's
wife. She smoked and sometimes her language was...um...colorful. After the
meeting, a senior pastor of a church who had 150 students attending pulled
his students from my talks for the rest of the conference because he was
angry at my remarks about my wife. For the rest of the conference, he met
with his students in a separate room when I was speaking. The minister was
concerned that the teenagers in his church might believe that ministers'
wives were not perfect. When I managed to find him and talk with him, he
was furious: "How dare you tell students a minister's wife smokes and uses
questionable language?" I looked at him and said as gently as I could,
"Because she does. It's the truth. I'm telling the truth; isn't that what the
gospel is all about?" He was not convinced. He didn't mind me telling the
truth; he did mind me suggesting a minister's wife might not be holy and
perfect.

The irony of the story, though, is that my audacity, which the senior
pastor had thought would turn his students from Christ, did the opposite.
Almost 10 years later, I ran into one of the sponsors of the event, and we
reminisced. "Mike," he said, "I'm glad to see you. I want to tell you what
happened to some students from the group that wasn't allowed to hear you.
About 20 teenagers from this group snuck out of the meetings led by their

I had been scheduled to speak at a denominational youth weekend out West, and about
two weeks prior to the event, I received a phone call from a woman on the design team
who wanted to review some conference schedules and travel plans. All in all it was
pretty routine. That was when she added this additional word of preparation:
*Please, when you give your talks, we've decided as a design team to ask that
you not mention the name of Jesus. We don't mind if you talk about God; in fact,
we hope you will. But we hope you'll understand that talking about Jesus will
offend some of our students, and we don't want to do anything that will make
them feel uncomfortable...*
And you know what? They were right! They were afraid to let the cat out of the bag
because people might misunderstand. But this wasn't about letting the cat out of the
bag; it was about letting the lion of Judah out of his cage.
God, however, is not so dainty in his revelations. As we see in Acts 2:1-13, God's
presence, like the proverbial "bull in a china shop," or more accurately, like a "violent
wind" in the temple, is disruptive, confusing, bewildering, almost comical...and utterly
amazing!

—Duffy Robbins

minister and came to yours anyway. At the end of the week, when you asked if anyone wanted to become a Christian, every single one of those 20 came forward."

The minister had misunderstood me. He thought I was giving the wrong impression about minister's wives. Instead I was giving the right impression about Jesus and his love for imperfect people. I wasn't justifying smoking and colorful language; I was celebrating God's grace. The minister didn't get the message, but his students did. Here was a minister who should have been celebrating that students wanted to know God. Instead he was criticizing.

When our ministries are audacious, many will be confused. They will think we mean one thing when we mean another: "Though seeing, they do not see; though hearing, they do not hear or understand" (Matthew 13:13). Many are afraid to tell the truth because they don't want to be misunderstood. We, however, should speak the truth audaciously, knowing that many will not understand.

There is rejection.

Many people in the church who misunderstand audacious ministry are more concerned about rules, policies, and biblical principles than they are about the unbelievable, miraculous, spectacular, unprecedented, once-in-a-lifetime event that occurs when someone does real ministry. Many of the people who witnessed Jesus' miracles did not rejoice; they were critical, cynical, and downright rude. When God is at work making people well, the sickness of those around them is exposed, and many people don't like that. They also don't like changing the way they think about those who were sick.

One audacious youth worker was rejected for reaching more teenagers. This junior high youth worker noticed that more and more of the kids coming to his youth group had not been reared in the church. A friend invited a friend who invited her friends until a large group of nonreligious, nonchurched students were attending youth group. Many of them smoked. There was a nonsmoking policy at youth group, of course, but they were allowed to smoke outside during the Bible study time that summer. One warm Sunday evening, while a few of the students were sitting on the lawn in front of the church, a board member walked by and saw one of them smoking while reading his Bible. He called an urgent board meeting, and the youth worker was told that smoking during Bible study was not appropriate behavior for students from this church. The youth worker tried to explain that a student smoking while studying the Bible was better than a student just smoking. But the board disagreed; they didn't want any teenagers smoking on church grounds, even if they were there to meet God.

Unfortunately, the youth worker didn't last long at the church because he had audacity. He was reaching those who had not been reached; he was teaching these kids to become disciples. These church members weren't interested in the messy process of developing disciples, though. They forgot that even Christ's disciples weren't perfect. They forgot that Christ reached out to the prostitutes, tax collectors, and smokers, so as the Pharisees rejected Christ, these church members fired this youth worker for being audacious. And they lost a valuable ministry.

If our ministries are audacious, we will be criticized, we will be scrutinized, and we will be rejected. Audacious, edgy ministry will always result in a gloriously tumultuous ministry—one very much like Christ's. Woo hoo!

There is courage.

Facing rejection and persecution takes courage. Obviously Jesus had courage, and his disciples were brave enough to challenge political and religious leaders. Daily, missionaries and youth workers face the dangers of the surrounding environments: the inner city, hostile governments, and terrorist groups. They all have the courage to do God's work, though, to develop creative ministries even when they are rejected. As youth workers we must convince students that they, too, can do God's work and that they have much to offer.

I've told this story in my book *Messy Spirituality*, but I think it's worth repeating here. It is a story about a student with amazing audacity; his courage kept us from a very unpleasant detainment. A number of years ago, our church youth group traveled to Mexico to build houses, and we wanted a big moving truck to take some materials with us. Most truck rental companies don't allow renters to take the trucks into Mexico because moving trucks are easy to steal. However, the owner of the local truck rental company in our small town agreed to let us take a truck into Mexico. He trusted us— after all, we were building houses for Jesus. We filled our rented truck with clothes, building supplies, tents, food, and tools.

Once we crossed the border of Mexico, we headed for the federal toll highway between Tijuana and Ensenada. After paying the toll, we noticed a group of federal police parked on the side of the road. As we passed them, three tough-looking young policemen, each holding a large machine gun, waved us over. They approached our truck and asked me to step out of the cab. Standing in front of them, I realized how big and menacing those machine guns were. The officer in the middle spoke in Spanish, and one of our group members translated his short speech: "We are taking your truck. Please move out of the way." Apparently, he was aware that many American rental companies did not allow their trucks in Mexico, so he was trying to scare us into giving him the truck. We pleaded with him not to confiscate our truck, explaining that we were building houses for the poor, and we were doing this for Jesus. The more we talked, though, the more demanding the officer became.

Suddenly, a 16-year-old foreign exchange student from Chile interrupted our stilted conversation with the officer. Politely but firmly, I took the young man aside and explained to him the seriousness of the situation. "Look," I said, "I know you want to help, but these soldiers are angry and they have machine guns."

"Oh, I've seen lots of machine guns in our country," he replied confidently, unruffled by my warning. Before I could stop him, he grabbed the rental contract, walked over to the men, and began yelling at the officer in the middle, waving his hands and frantically pointing to the contract. Then he actually pushed his finger into the soldier's chest. At that point I knew we were all headed for a Mexican jail.

But I was wrong. The more the boy yelled, the more sheepish the federal guardsman looked, until, exasperated, he stopped the boy with a loud, "VAMOS!"

Immediately the boy turned to me and said, "Get in the truck. Let's get out of here before he changes his mind." We jumped into the truck and drove off in a cloud of dust. As we fled the scene, I asked this young exchange student what he'd said to the guard that made him change his mind. "I pointed to the contract and told him it said the truck was legal in Mexico and that he would be in a lot of trouble if we lost our truck," he replied happily.

"But the contract doesn't say that," I objected.

"I know, but the officer couldn't read English!" he told me.

Now the young Chilean didn't act very spiritually—he lied! But he was also bold, courageous, and street smart. And that is the moral of the story: be audacious, have courage.

CORE Reality: Audacity

Youth ministry is exciting because teenagers respond to Jesus. students are looking for excitement, adventure, danger, and risk. Jesus, by the very nature of his presence, makes that happen. teenagers want to be courageous, and if we provide Jesus, the adventure will take care of itself. As Thomas Merton said, "Be careful if you're thinking of making friends with the Holy Spirit—because he's going to ask you to die!" (quoted in *Too Deep for Words*, Thelma Hall. Paulist Press, 1988. p. 24). Jesus was audacious, and if we follow him, we will be, too. Our youth ministries will look messy and be misunderstood; they will be rejected because we do things differently; and they will have the most creative and courageous people in the church.

MANDATE: Youth ministry must push students, parents, and the church outside their comfort zones.

CHAPTER FIVE

CORE REALITY

HUMILITY

PHILIPPIANS 2:1-11

1 CORINTHIANS 1:26-2:5

1 PETER 5:5-6

MICAH 6:8

Mike's Story

A quiet man mentored me. He spent his life on the sidelines and in the shadows while those into whom he poured his life took center stage. Very few people notice him, and he enjoys his anonymity. Behind his quiet exterior is an incredibly observant mind, capable of seeing potential in others. In the 40 years I have known him, he has dedicated himself to helping, advising, and placing potential leaders in the church and in the public arena. His wisdom and keen sensitivity have enabled him to minister to hundreds of leaders all over the world. His influence is impossible to measure, but I'm sure it's mind-boggling.

Jim Slevcove noticed me at a youth camp when I was 18. Sneaking up behind me, he offered me a job at a large conference center, which, coupled with his mentoring, launched me into ministry. Jim believed in Wayne Rice and me when few did, and he found ways to support us as we began Youth Specialties.

Jim Slevcove is a sweet, humble Russian man who silently decreases so Jesus can increase. Very few people notice him. But God notices. Even today, in his 70s, Jim manages to empower and guide potential leaders so they can make a difference. I'm guessing that behind every one of us in ministry is a humble, godly person, like Jim, who believes in us and willingly stays in the background so we can do ministry.

Humility means gentle, meek, without arrogance, unassuming, unpretentious, kind, unassertive, quiet. Youth workers should have humility. We should always search for ways to decrease so that Jesus can increase. In fact, John the Baptist models this when, asked why he wasn't upset that his followers were now following Jesus, he says, "He must become greater; I must become less" (John 3:30).

Most of us think of humility as a positive value, a quality of character to be sought after by all who want to live an exemplary life, a life patterned after Jesus. We take humility for granted, as though it has always been a socially desirable quality. But humility is a biblical value, and it wasn't always considered a positive value.

Paul wrote about humility in his letters to the churches. There is a rea-

John the Baptist was human, but not ordinary. He didn't look like a priest; he didn't sound like a preacher; and he probably didn't smell like a saint (whatever saints smell like). He was not the light. He was bearing witness to the light. He was useful but never considered himself indispensable.

Later in the gospel of John, the Baptist is described as being the friend of the bridegroom. In those days one of the jobs of the friend of the bridegroom was to take the hands of the groom and the hands of the bride and bring them together and then fade into the background.

That describes our job as youth workers. We are to take the hands of students and bring them to the hands of God and then fade into the background. Youth workers should be looking for ways that they may decrease so that Jesus can increase.

—*Les Christie*

son for this: Paul wrote to Gentile churches that were primarily from a Greek culture. This emerging church was new, different, strange, alien, radical, and counter cultural; the church in Ephesus was inventing what it meant to follow Christ. These people were explorers, and each step took them to new ground, places no one had been before. Therefore, when Paul writes to the church at Ephesus, he's doing more than giving advice; he's clarifying the differences between the Greek way of living and the new way, Christ's way. As far as Greeks were concerned, they were the center of civilization: everyone should learn to speak their language; the rich were more important than the poor; and although brilliant and refined, they were cruel and merciless to those who were different from them. The poor, the aged, the weak of body and mind, the animals, the children, and the women were pushed to the fringe of society, ignored, or, worse, eliminated. It was survival of the fittest. Because of this, humility was not valued in Greek culture; it was a weakness. In the Greek language there was no word for *humility* because it was a negative characteristic, a characteristic of weakness—a cowering, cringing, servile, ignoble quality.

This is why Paul's words to the Ephesians were strange, shocking, and difficult for the people to understand. He was not only talking about a new way of living, but he also was talking about a way of living that was the complete opposite of the way they had been taught:

> *Be completely humble and gentle; be patient, bearing with one another in love. Make every effort to keep the unity of the Spirit through the bond of peace...*
> (Ephesians 4:2-3)

These are outrageous words for a people who had never lived this way before. Being a Christian was a completely new way of life. Here Paul lists the five radical characteristics of Christians: humility, gentleness, patience, love, and peace. These five characteristics, he says, will make Christians stand apart from others.

In our culture humility is generally not considered a virtue; instead we're all about self-promotion, power, popularity, and outward appearances. Unfortunately, these values have found their way into the church, and the result is the church placing people in positions of leadership for all the wrong reasons: elders whose primary qualifications seem to be their bank accounts or deacons who get appointed because of their political power.

But then I look at the way I've placed both adult and student leaders in my youth ministry over the years. Far too often I've recruited for coolness, popularity, athletic ability, or youthfulness instead of Christ-like humility. I wonder what would happen if I made a humble spirit the primary criteria for recruiting adult and student leaders. Christ reminds us that he came "to serve rather than to be served." How counter-cultural am I really willing to be?

—*Marv Penner*

Today we give lip service to humility, outwardly claiming it is a desirable quality, but the truth is that humility is not valued in our culture. We celebrate people like Mother Teresa because she is so unusual; very few people want to be like her, and her death marked the end of the age of humility. Princess Di's death and funeral, however, reflect our culture's obsession with strength, power, beauty, and talent. The power of the gospel in the Greek culture, in our culture, and in every culture is the *power to transform humility from a negative characteristic into a positive one.*

In a day when we elevate and admire youth workers with dazzling gifts and talents, it's nice to know that Jesus still elevates and admires the same value he's always admired—humility. God is seeking those youth workers willing to serve and follow him. He is looking for soft clay, ready to be molded by his hand. Therefore, by modeling servanthood, by being humble, youth workers point students to the "name that is above every name": Jesus Christ. Here are some things we can do to develop humility in ourselves and in our youth groups.

Be dependent.

What?! We are supposed to be the ones who have it all together so our kids can depend on us. Aren't we supposed to walk into youth group with all the answers? I mean, our marriages are perfect, our lives are perfect, and our relationships with God are perfect. Well, uh…not exactly.

Of course we are happy to admit the transforming power of Jesus; we are excited to announce that "once we were blind and now we can see," and we understand that when we were blind, we had many other flaws and weak-

> The day of the personality-driven, center-of-attention, bigger-than-life youth worker is over! There was a time when those qualities were the only ones churches looked for in youth workers. (Even today some attempt to hang on to that era.)
>
> But healthy churches and youth workers are realizing that leadership has to be turned over to a team of followers who have dedicated themselves to the spiritual life of the community. This team includes adults, parents, church leaders, and, most importantly, teenagers. As they work together and depend on each other, they model humility. Rather than having Jesus' mission submit to them, they submit themselves to the mission of Jesus; they depend on him.
>
> —Charley Scandlyn

nesses as well. But it is harder to admit that many of those flaws are still with us. God healed our blindness and is working on the rest of us. We depend on him because we are not perfect. We must admit our fallibility, recognize our brokenness, and realize that God is our strength because we are weak.

Good youth workers are apprehensive, unsure whether they are adequate for the jobs they are given; good youth workers feel helpless because they recognize they are weak. Remember the people who made a difference in your life. My hunch is that they weren't dazzling, gifted, amazing people. Rather, they were probably unimpressive, ordinary men and women who gave what they had, loved as best they could, and pointed you in the direction of Jesus. It wasn't their youth, their good looks, their coolness that made a difference; it was their faithfulness, love, and willingness to rely on God.

God works in and through our helplessness. He is not frustrated by our lack of skill, by our ordinariness; in fact, he relishes our dependence on him. After 42 years of ministry, I'm convinced that helplessness what is endears us to God. When we admit we are weak and have flaws, God can enter us—he can support us. Jesus didn't attempt to convert the Pharisees and Sadducees

After six years as a youth pastor in Berkeley, I moved to Southern California, and I felt God's call to work with inner-city youth. Almost immediately, I was transformed from "youth ministry expert" to "youth ministry novice" because these kids had needs I had no experience with. None of my seminars or books could help me. And it was the best thing that happened to my ministry career.

Such transitions are God's plan for spiritual growth. The less you know, the more open you are to God...because God has less of your agenda to contend with.

—*Laurie Polich*

or choose the most gifted and talented people for disciples; apparently he needed the least qualified disciples he could find: a tax collector, a zealot, and fishermen. Tax collectors didn't know anything about gentleness, kindness, and unconditional love; they were traitors because they collected taxes for the occupying army and would do anything to make a profit. Zealots routinely killed tax collectors, and fishermen were not exactly known for finesse and public diplomacy. Jesus took a bunch of ragged, unimpressive, inadequate, and unlikely men for discipleship. And through them God turned the world upside down. Similarly, when you and I give up trying to improve our skills and depend on Jesus, then God can really use us.

Youth work is not about our talents and gifts; it's about our honesty to admit our lack of talent and our courage to recognize we can't do it alone. The rich young ruler was honest, but he didn't have the courage to give up his wealth and rely on Jesus (Luke 18:18-30). Humility gives us the courage to let go of our weaknesses and depend on God so he can do amazing things in the lives of our students.

Be teachable.

When we admit that we are fallible and need to depend on God, we can become teachable. If we are teachable, we are always ready to know more, to change, to adapt, and to restructure. We must read, study, take classes, get a mentor, and learn from teenagers as well as adults. We may have a clear philosophy of ministry, but if we recognize we are fallible and must depend on God, we also recognize when our philosophy doesn't work. If we are teachable, we can be taught that the kids have changed, the culture has changed, or we have changed since we began, and, thus, our ministries need to change. From here we can learn new ways to do youth ministry because the word *new* does not strike terror in our hearts.

Most of us parents have no problem recognizing our need to be teachable. The longer we're parents, the more we realize how much we don't know. During the years that Tim Smith was writing a book on parenting, he realized his need to be taught. Before he even had children, Tim decided he wanted to write a book on parenting, which he would title *How to Raise Your Kids.* After his children were born, he changed the working title to *Ideas on How to Raise Kids.* When his children grew older, he again changed the title to *Tips from a Fellow Struggler.* Finally, after his children became teenagers, he called his book *Anybody Have Any Ideas?* Good parents and good youth workers recognize how much they don't know and are not afraid to ask, "Do you have any ideas?"

Here are some practical ways to keep yourself in a teachable mode.

Read the Bible on a regular basis. Promise yourself you will not read the Bible just for youth group or Bible studies. Find an adult Bible study that will encourage you to apply what you read to your own life, not just to your students' lives.

Read books for your soul. Ask people you respect what books they have read lately. Continually update your library and develop a list of authors whose books minister to you as an adult, not to you as a youth worker.

Keep yourself current. Find out as much as you can about world events, as well as youth-related events, programs, fads, and popular culture.

Learn from your students. Ask them questions, give them opportunities to teach, write, and lead, so you can learn from and about them as well.

Take every opportunity you can to get training. Attend seminars, conventions, and one-day training sessions so you can learn new skills and develop new ideas. Also, at these meetings you will be affirmed and rejuvenated by being with other youth workers.

Often you learn more from the people attending the training than from the trainers themselves.

Use the Internet. The Internet is a great resource for sharing ideas, learning new ones, and chatting with other youth workers. Search the Web for resources such as books, ideas, meetings, conferences, and even concerts.

When we allow ourselves to be taught, not only do we grow spiritually, but our students also see modeled a desire to learn and grow. The more we admit we need to learn, the more God can teach us, and the more he can use us.

Be accessible.

When our students see that we, like them, are still learning, they will be more comfortable approaching us. This is a simple definition of *humility*— accessibility. That means available, open, present, reachable. If we are accessible, there are no obstacles keeping students from approaching us, connecting with us, being with us. Some youth workers give a lot of time to their kids, and they make it clear that their time is all they can have. Giving them access to our time is good, but access to our time is meaningless without making ourselves accessible because humility is not about how much time we give, but how much of *ourselves* we give. Making ourselves accessible to students by being adults who will listen and share is more important than

Often God urges me to share my difficulties and shortcomings with students during my teaching time. Early in my ministry, I resisted the nudgings: *What will my kids think? Will they still listen to me? Will I disappoint them?*

Taking the plunge was frightening, but I started by sharing that from the fifth grade into my adult years, I was teased about my weight. Following that talk, the students sat quietly in a line, waiting to share their stories of pain with me.

"I never knew you struggled with that, Heather!" one said.

"You know when you talked about being compared to Miss Piggy? That same thing happened to me last year..." another admitted.

When I shared my own struggles, my own fear, and my own brokenness, I became accessible.

—Heather Flies

the content of our programs or the amount of time we spend working.

One of the most startling and radical aspects of Jesus Christ is that he was approachable. Obviously most religious leaders were (and often still are) not approachable; they were distant, segregated, and isolated from others. At first Jesus' followers expected him to be like everyone else, which is why they tried to keep people away from him. Luckily, Jesus wasn't like everyone else, he was reachable—he modeled humility.

Be flexible.

Humility means we're flexible, so in addition to being accessible to our students, we need to be able to adapt to their needs. We need to be sensitive to what God is doing, and we must recognize there's an agenda more important than ours. Some youth workers believe it is their job to finish the lesson, cover the entire curriculum, get through the program, and end on time. But this doesn't always work with what the students need. Being flexible means we are willing to change or drop the lesson if a more important issue comes up. Inflexibility is blindly adhering to a plan or agenda that has become obsolete or irrelevant, and it breeds contempt as well as frustration.

Inflexability creates a distance between students and ourselves. For years our youth group traveled to Mexico to build houses for the poor with Amor Ministries. It's always difficult to find a good cooking crew because spending a week fixing meals for 200 people in primitive conditions is hard work. Fortunately, we found two women who were willing to spend hours planning and coordinating menus and meals every year. Each year, though, they became more rigid and inflexible; they were committed to nutritional and healthy meals at any price, and they wouldn't listen to what we wanted. The kids' complaints about the food increased every year until the complaints couldn't be ignored. We tried pointing out to the cooks that huge amounts of food were being wasted because the teenagers weren't eating. We also noticed that they were buying junk food by the truckload at small little markets in the Mexican areas where we worked, defeating the cooks' own desire to give them nutritional food: their meals were incredibly healthy, but no one was eating them. When we asked if they could compromise and make meals the people liked such as tacos, steak, or spaghetti, their answer was "No, absolutely not." So instead of eating the healthy food that was cooked,

I can't count the number of youth workers who have quoted Matthew 10:19 to me (although most don't know the reference) as a biblical excuse for not planning their teaching for the evening: "I don't have to worry about what I am going to say," they argue. "God will give me the words when I need them." These youth workers believe it's almost more spiritual to *not* plan. This stuns me. (Matthew 10 says that when you're arrested for preaching the gospel and flogged in the synagogue, you don't have to worry about what you will say—flogging would tend to cloud the mind—because God will give you the words.) Luke 14:28-33 gives us two wonderful pictures that tell us a little pre-planning can go a long way toward ensuring the success of our adventures.

Here's a thought: *the key to flexibility is good planning.* If you want to be flexible, to go with the flow, to allow creativity to flourish, then try planning well in advance. This will do two things for your ministry: it will allow other leaders to participate with you, and it will enable you to be as spontaneous as you choose since you have a plan to fall back on if the creativity dries up.

—Dan Jessup

the students were eating food that was even unhealthier than what we asked the cooks to provide. The cooks' agenda had become more important than the needs of the campers.

So we hired new cooks. The complaints stopped, and the compliments began. Meals became the most anticipated part of the day, and kids stopped buying junk food. At first, cooking for our camp was not a glamorous job, but when we hired cooks who were flexible, who were willing to serve the needs of the people, it actually became a highly appreciated job. At the end of every camp, instead of grumbling and complaining, the campers gave the cooks a standing ovation. During the week the new cooks developed relationships with the campers and were able to talk with them about Jesus because they were flexible—they were humble.

Be decreased.

When we are accessible and flexible, our own importance will decrease. After all, it's about God and our students, not us. As our own sense of importance decreases, we'll become small, little, and tiny. Then it will be easier for us to stay out of God's way. If, because we appear big and strong, teenagers depend on us for their relationship to God, they will never depend on God for themselves. When we fail, their relationships with God will fail. It is our desire that students become independently dependent on God.

One school of spirituality, founded in the seventeenth century, based its

One of the ways I've found that increases the effectiveness of my teaching and speaking (while I "decrease" in the process) is using the stories of my students as illustrations. As I take the time to get to know my students, it's not long before I'm learning about experiences in their lives that can powerfully illustrate biblical principles such as courage, forgiveness, perseverance in suffering, boldness, dealing with temptation, or finding God's will.

—*Marv Penner*

philosophies on valuing the small contributions of a person rather than the obvious ones. The Salesian school emphasized the significance of the little things. The Salesians point out that although we aren't always able to give God great things, we can offer God, continuously and with great love, little things. It focused on the "little virtues" that were based on three crucial qualities: humility, simplicity, and gentleness. Being decreased means practicing the little virtues instead of focusing on the ones that usually get more attention. In our youth ministries these little virtues are praying for, affirming, listening to, writing letters and e-mails to, hanging out with, attending performances by, tutoring, and spending time with our students. Very few people other than the students notice these actions; compared to our sermons, camps, and group meetings, these little virtues appear diminished. To do these, we have to be humble. These actions don't bring us recognition; they decrease us in the eyes of others. However, we must trust that the little virtues we practice will help teenagers bump into God's great love without us getting in the way. In fact, we'd be too small to get in the way—decreased.

We have no better model for this than the one Paul gives us in his letter to the church at Corinth:

> *When I came to you, brothers, I did not come with eloquence or superior wisdom as I proclaimed to you the testimony about God. For I resolved to know nothing while I was with you except Jesus Christ and him crucified. I came to you in weakness and fear, and with much trembling. My message and my preaching were not with wise and persuasive words, but with a demonstration of the Spirit's power, so that your faith might not rest on men's wisdom, but on God's power.*

(1 Corinthians 2:1-5)

Even though Paul had the gift of eloquence and incredible speaking power, he chose to be decreased so Jesus could be increased. He used little virtues in his relationships with the church at Corinth, rather than his obvious ones. Determined not to get in God's way, Paul humbled himself so those he ministered to could meet Christ. When we allow our own importance to decrease, we can be used to point the way to God.

Be nobody.

Youth workers are often the most unappreciated group of people in ministry. In many churches, they are last on the list of budget priorities and first on the list of departments to be cut. Youth workers often find themselves torn between the conflicting expectations of parents, church boards, pastors, students, and themselves, and it is very easy for youth workers to develop inferiority complexes, to become insecure, and to begin to doubt their calling. This is all the more likely if they are working to decrease their importance in the lives of their students so that God can increase in importance.

Feeling like a nobody can be even more developed in volunteer youth workers. Because they volunteer (a position title that implies "this is a position no one else wants" or "we don't think the job is important enough to pay someone for it"), they often feel as if they are not qualified, are not the best people for the job, and can't really relate to teenagers. I am always shocked by how many youth workers admit they feel inferior and inadequate.

Well, guess what? They're in good company. Most of us feel inadequate. Most of us feel inferior. Many of us look at ourselves as too old, too fat, and too uncool. Most of us feel ordinary and worry that we are just nobodies trying to do somebody's job. And to be honest, our feelings might just be true. Some of us are not young, not skinny, and not cool. We really

I burned out after two years of youth ministry. It was humbling. I was young, just out of seminary, and ready to show the church how things should be done! But I was immature, and it wasn't long before I became the center of my ministry. I had built the student ministry on my charisma, my enthusiasm, my creativity. Do you hear the recurring word? Yes…it's *my*.

After two short years I had nothing left to give, and I left the church. Sadly, it took the youth group several years to recover when I left "my" ministry. Through humbling experiences like this, I've learned that without "me"—when I become invisible—the ministry survives and actually thrives. This happens when a leader learns to build into a team of people, young and old.

—*Helen Musick*

I love those words of the apostle Paul in 1 Corinthians 2:1-5. I get so intimidated that effective youth ministry is all about how much I know, how skilled I am, how hip I am (or am not!). And then I read Paul's words, "weakness...fear...trembling"—and I think, "You know what? I can do that!"

God's strength is made perfect in our weakness. He has always used the improbable to do the impossible. Effective youth ministry is not about infallible people lifting up the name of Jesus. It is about an infallible Jesus lifting up flawed people who are willing to trust him.

—Duffy Robbins

are nobodies. But here is the good news: Jesus doesn't care. Jesus loves nobodies. Jesus chooses nobodies. D. L. Moody, a great evangelist, explained the phenomenon of discovering one is a nobody: "Moses spent forty years thinking he was somebody; then he spent forty years on the back side of the desert realizing he was nobody; finally, he spent the last forty years learning what God can do with a nobody" (quoted in *Wisdom for the Way*, Gordon S. Jackson. NavPress, 2000. p. 93). Wow! Moses was a nobody, too. That is humility. Thank God for nobodies because the history of the church is filled with nobodies who totally changed the world. It is amazing what God can do with a humble nobody.

Think about it. Youth workers are nothing more than a ragtag, foolish, unsophisticated, unfinished, and disrespected group of nobodies who have been called to work with a ragtag, foolish, unsophisticated, unfinished, and disrespected group of nobodies called adolescents.

What an honor!

What a calling!

CORE Reality: Humility

We have been called to our work in a church culture that often evaluates us by competency, efficiency, productivity, activity, homogeneity, and conformity. All this amounts to being judged by one primary criterion: the number of students in our youth groups. But we serve a Jesus who judges us by a completely different standard: incompetence, inefficiency, intimacy, inactivity, diversity, and nonconformity. All of this amounts to Christ asking us to fulfill one primary criterion: **giving ourselves**.

We have been called by a Jesus who is not impressed by large, razzle-dazzle ministries, but by a Jesus who celebrates even the small ones. He rejects power in favor of powerlessness; he chooses the lost rather than the found, the loser over the winner, the imperfect over the perfect. God uses those who are humble.

Jesus is the one who invited us to crash the party of youth ministry. No one would have invited us otherwise; we're lowly, underpaid, and unrecognized. Jesus is the one who gave us the VIP pass to get into ministry; he's the one who caused us to quit our good-paying jobs, to take our families of four or two or six and scrape by. He chose us—dependant nobodies who need to be taught, who need to learn to be flexible and small, and who are so incapable. But because we have been called, we are the privileged ones. We are lucky enough, privileged enough, and graced enough to be called youth workers. And we are honored to be called, glad to be with Jesus, graced to be the church, privileged to cast our lot with the teenagers of this culture and introduce them to Jesus Christ. Most of all we are eager to decrease so that he may increase.

MANDATE: Youth ministry must be clothed in humility.

CHAPTER SIX

CORE REALITY

DIVERSITY

GALATIANS 3:27-28

1 TIMOTHY 4:12

REVELATION 7:9-10

1 CORINTHIANS 12:12-31

Mike's Story

At the first National Youth Workers Convention in 1970, one of the general session speakers said in the middle of his talk, "We don't need to take the kid out of the ghetto; we just need to take the ghetto out of his heart." Before the sound of his words had ended, a black Young Life leader jumped up and yelled "Bullsh—!" Tense dialogue ensued and overflowed out of the session, into the hallways of the hotel, and eventually into our churches. Urban ministry was in its infancy, and at that moment we were forced to admit we were infants ourselves when it came to dealing with diversity. It was obvious we could not ignore the urban church any longer, and we could not ignore diversity.

Unfortunately, we haven't made much progress. We love the idea of diversity, but we don't seem to love the practice of it.

We don't talk much about diversity in youth ministry today, but in the late '60s and early '70s, diversity was central to the Jesus Movement. Because the Jesus Movement was revolutionary, it threatened the status quo, criticized the church for its lack of inclusiveness, and called the church to lead the American culture toward diversity rather than imitate the exclusiveness of the current culture.

We believe diversity is a CORE reality of youth ministry (all ministry, actually). We didn't come to this realization because of political correctness; we came to it from reading the Bible. Diversity is all over Scripture. Jesus rubbed his culture's nose in diversity. Every time he told a story, the hero was a Samaritan, a sort of Jewish half-breed. Full-blooded Jewish folks hated Samaritans. Jesus knew this and seemed to love saying, "and he was a Samaritan." But prejudice wasn't a problem only for the Jews; in the early church it was a huge problem. That is why Paul's words to the Galatians had such power: "There is neither Jew nor Greek, slave nor free, male nor female, for you are all one in Christ Jesus" (Galatians 3:28). To the Galatians his words were beyond radical; they were shocking, strange, alien, and revolutionary. Sadly, they are just as shocking, strange, alien, and revolutionary today.

There is one point in all of Christianity when the church experienced true harmony and unity—Acts 2:42-47. We all know it because we quote it any time we are dissatisfied with our current church experience. We start longing for that first-century church community where we all grow, share, serve, have everything in common, and watch numbers increase daily.

Well, guess what? That was the beginning of the book of Acts, not the end. The rest of the book (in fact the rest of the New Testament and the rest of the history of the church) is a long, painful, and difficult struggle as it becomes more diverse. First everything is totally harmonious, and then they heal a beggar. Next they reach out to an Ethiopian eunuch. After that it's a Roman Centurion. Then, of course, there are the Gentiles. Harmony is out and the struggle of diversity is in!

People start getting arrested, lives are threatened, and at the end of Acts, everything is unsettled. Yet this was Paul's battle. Peter also recognized that this was the direction of the true church: to be a light to all nations and tribes, regardless of the struggle!

—*Charley Scandlyn*

It would have been great if the civil rights movement had been led by all churches, but it wasn't. Only a minority of churches and ministers called the rest of the world to diversity. Much of the civil rights language was God language, church language, and the language of the old Negro spirituals. For its full impact, read aloud Dr. Martin Luther King, Jr.'s 1963 speech, a speech we should never forget:

So let freedom ring from the prodigious hilltops of New Hampshire. Let freedom ring from the mighty mountains of New York. Let freedom ring from the heightening Alleghenys of Pennsylvania. Let freedom ring from the snowcapped Rockies of Colorado. Let freedom ring from the curvaceous slopes of California. But not only that, let freedom ring from Stone Mountain of Georgia. Let freedom ring from Lookout Mountain of Tennessee. Let freedom ring from every hill and molehill of Mississippi, from every mountainside. When we allow freedom to ring from every city, every citizen, every hamlet, from every state and every city, we will be able to speed up that day when all of God's children, black men and white men, Jews and gentiles, Protestants and Catholics, will be able to join hands and sing in the words of the old Negro spiritual, "Free at last! Free at last! Thank God Almighty, we are free at last!"

(Transcribed from *In Remembrance of Martin*. PBS video, 2002)

Wow! What a speech! What a truth! What a CORE reality! And King is simply paraphrasing Galatians 3:28. His words were true in 1963, and they are true today because racial hatred is *increasing*, not decreasing. To combat this the church should model, should live, diversity.

Of the nine CORE realities, diversity is the most uncomfortable and the most difficult to live, but we must. The church should be known for its diversity, and our youth groups should be hotbeds of diversity and examples

Because many of our current images of biblical characters are European, we have lost the great ethnic diversity of the Bible. In fact, the Bible is probably the most multiethnic story any of us will ever read. If we were to teach about the true ethnicity of many of the Old Testament characters, we would be telling the stories of Africans, Asians, and many different middle-Eastern ethnicities. Many biblical heroes could have looked like those many of us see as national enemies today. As presented in Acts 2, the first Christian church was comprised of a multiethnic group of Jews from every nation under Heaven. Our traditional depictions of a pale-skinned Jesus should be confronted with the multiethnic Jesus who died and rose for all of humanity.

—Efrem Smith

of inclusiveness, leading the church to practice what it preaches. However, the church is weak on this point, and what concerns us most about diversity in modern youth ministry is how many youth workers don't notice their youth groups aren't diverse. Even if youth workers notice the lack of diversity in their groups, they seem perfectly satisfied without it. Here are the comments we hear most often:

1. We would love to be diverse, but we don't live in a diverse area.
2. We've tried, but the adults complained, and they pay the bills.
3. We tried, and the white kids dropped out, which caused the parents to drop out, which caused the pastor to pay me a visit. Now I've dropped out.
4. We have invited other ethnic groups, but they say our programs are too white.
5. We invite them, but they don't have the transportation to get here.
6. We tried to invite them, but our events are too expensive.

All of these comments are excuses. Each one is based on an obstacle that can be overcome. Granted, overcoming some obstacles could lead to being fired, but many good and righteous actions lead to being fired. We

Our students live in an ever-increasing multiethnic and multicultural world. My town (Minneapolis, Minnesota) is an example of a flourishing multiethnic, multicultural world. Based on information from the 2000 census report, Minnesota has one of the fastest growing Latino populations in the country, the second largest Southeast Asian population in the country, and, outside of Somalia, the largest Somali population in the world.

Despite this growing diversity, Minnesota, like most other states, has a very racially segregated church community. Sunday at 11 a.m. is likely the most segregated hour in my state—and sadly, in just about every other state, too. How can we talk about Heaven as a place of many nations, peoples, languages, and tribes (Revelation 7) while the church remains the most segregated institution in the country? How can we prepare students to share their faith in their circle of influence—i.e., more and more multiethnic and multicultural—without us taking radical steps in the area of diversity?

—Efrem Smith

can, however, work with what we have been given; there are ways in which each obstacle can be hurdled:

1. Befriend a church from a different area.
2. Get the adults involved in creating diversity.
3. Discuss the need for diversity with the pastor and church board.
4. Ask people from different ethnic groups what would make them feel more comfortable and change the program.
5. Raise money for transportation.
6. Raise money for event and camp scholarships.

There are ministries all over the country that are making an effort to diversify, and they are experiencing the blessings that come from a diverse youth group. When we value diversity, we find a way to make it happen; it's that simple. This doesn't mean, though, that every youth group has a perfect mix of races or youth subcultures; what it does mean is that youth groups push the envelope and find ways (even little ways) to move closer to diversity.

Youth Specialties believes, and has always believed, "Something is better than nothing." So if you are in a church where diversity is never mentioned and you start mentioning it, you are "making it happen." If your youth group has never connected with an urban church or urban project and now does once a year, you are "making it happen." When we work toward diversity, we search it out and we aim for it. Any movement toward diversity and away from exclusivity is a good step.

These steps toward diversity encompass much more than ethnic differences, though. There are many types of diversity: economic, tribal, generational, and theological, just to name a few. Including as many different forms of diversity as possible in our youth groups is important, but before we focus on the various types of diversity we can include in our groups, we need to understand what diversity is.

Diversity is inclusive, not exclusive.

Inclusive is a politically charged word that creates anxiety in some who are afraid of what they don't know. Inclusive means bringing in new people, concepts, and ideas with which we are unfamiliar. If we don't understand them, we can't control them. Really, then, many people are afraid of diversity because they are afraid of losing *control*. But one of Jesus' main points is that we should give up control. It is more important to break down the barriers

> A friend from a prominent, historical church experienced "white flight." While the congregation had become mainly white senior citizens, the surrounding neighborhood looked totally different—and any students he brought in immediately felt disconnected from the church and wouldn't stay long.
>
> I suggested that he bring in teenagers from the neighborhood for a historical tour of the church. Then he could explain that the legacy of the church now belonged to them and that they could take their church to the next level by meeting the needs of the surrounding community. I also suggested that he bring in some of the older members, specifically successful businessmen and women, so some of the youth in the neighborhood could connect with them.
>
> The result was stronger community relationships, and that began to change the way both groups saw each other.
>
> —Fred Lynch

and set the captives free. Jesus made it clear everyone is welcome, everyone is included, everyone is loved by God, and everyone can respond to his love. Inclusiveness means the doors of our ministries are open to all: skaters, non-Christians, Asians, Hispanics, blacks, and gang members.

Of course, we must have boundaries limiting actions, but limiting actions is very different from limiting people. One youth group we know invites gang members (no limit on people) but has a rule: "Leave weapons at the door" (limit on actions). Youth workers should challenge themselves to think of ways they can include diverse groups, even when boundaries must be placed on their actions.

Diversity is valued, not tolerated.

Diversity is not tolerated, it's valued. It isn't something we put up with; it's something we desire. Diversity requires interaction, appreciation, understanding, and dialogue, and all of these take time. Genuine community doesn't happen overnight; bonding doesn't occur magically; relationships require time and space to take hold. Transformation of our prejudices is a slow process, but a process worth encouraging. If this process is encouraged, people will value the diversity of the group rather than simply tolerate it; they will realize it is necessary rather than simply politically correct.

In one youth group this process took a few years, but the result was worth it. A friend of mine inherited a youth group of kids who were of the same color, the same social class, and the same value system. After a large group of Cambodian refugees moved into the area, a number of Cambodian high school students started attending the youth group. Because the youth worker worked part time at the high school, he was able to befriend them during orientation, and they began to come to his youth group. The moment the Cambodians started coming, however, things began to change. Slowly, one by one, the white students dropped out until the makeup of the youth group was completely different. Now the fringe students, the unpopular ones, and the outsiders felt safe attending. The youth worker received a great deal of criticism for "not appreciating" the students who were in the group before and for "chasing away" the "good" ones.

What really happened, though, was that the previous group was uncomfortable with new people. The teenagers valued their sameness more than they valued diversity. Ironically, within a couple of years' time, the Cambodians, the fringe students, and the outsiders were involved in every area of the high school with the popular white students. Instead of tolerating the Cambodian students, the secular high school valued diversity, and the Cambodians responded by becoming part of the community. It took a few years, but the relationships that developed and the youth worker's willingness to continue, even when he was criticized, created a diverse community that valued others instead of tolerating them.

Diversity is intentional, not convenient.

Youth ministry can't ignore diversity any longer. Clearly, Scripture calls us to challenge prejudice. If we wait for it to happen, it won't. If we wait for "the right moment," there won't be one. The effort to develop diversity in our youth groups often has to be intentional, and at first it usually meets with resistance from kids, their parents, and even the church itself. In the movie *Remember the Titans,* an all-white high school football team has to accept a new black head coach and black players as well. The white and the black players have to sit together in the bus to football camp and room together. By the end of the movie, though, the Titan football team has been transformed into a team of friends. Uniting white and black players was intentional; the decision was made to have them play together, and there was resistance at first. No one waited until the timing was convenient, until the players wanted to. However, what was at first resisted was later accepted: athletes who were placed in an uncomfortable situation, who were asked to do something they wouldn't have chosen, became comfortable with their diversity. In the end they chose to live and play together.

It's not only important for us to talk to students about racism, but we also must expose them to it and equip them to dismantle it. In many ways the church actively addresses poverty and homelessness through ministries that put students on the front lines. If the church is going to address the issue of racism, then we must put teenagers on the front lines of reconciliation efforts (2 Corinthians 5:17-20).

—*Efrem Smith*

Of course life isn't a movie; diversity is not always accepted. However, the church should be known for its willingness to seek diversity; it should be known for intending to create diversity, not sitting back and waiting for it to happen conveniently.

Types of Diversity

Although there are numerous types of diversity, we mention the four—ethnic, tribal (youth subculture), mental and physical, as well as generational—below because we believe they are the ones most pertinent to youth groups today.

Ethnic diversity

Ethnic diversity is the American way of life; our Asian, Hispanic, black, Vietnamese, Samoan, Cambodian, and middle Eastern populations are growing. And so is racism. We can't ignore it, and we have to deal with it. However, we don't suggest establishing quotas for youth groups. What we do suggest, though, is intention—*seek diversity*. If our youth groups are not ethnically diverse, then we need to find ways to get them to interact with different ethnic and racial groups. As students get to know more about other cultures, they will learn to value diversity rather than just tolerate it, and our groups will become inclusive.

After some trying events two churches whose congregations were wary of diversity grew to value it. One of the churches was in the Deep South, and the youth worker in the church was concerned about the lingering racism. He decided to plan a summer mission trip to a black church in South Chicago. He was being intentional about including diversity in his youth group. Forty high school students signed up…until the parents discovered the project was in South Chicago. One by one the teenagers canceled until there were only 10 left.

Similarly, the black church in South Chicago was reluctant to host these students because they were from Florida. The assistant pastor of the South Chicago church, Abraham Lincoln Washington, had been arrested in Florida. Rev. Washington was on his way back from a vacation with his wife and daughter and stopped to get gas in a small, rural town. After Rev. Washington stretched his legs from the long trip, he sat on a park bench to relax before they continued the long journey home. While he was sitting there, someone called 911 to report a black man sitting on a park bench. Apparently in this town it is unlawful for a black person to sit on a bench.

A policeman arrived and began harassing Rev. Washington, asking him what he was doing there. Then, the policeman asked him for his name. "Abraham Lincoln Washington," he replied. The policeman was not amused: "Very funny, now what's your real name?" When Rev. Washington said it was his real name, the policeman grabbed him, wrestled him to the ground, and handcuffed him. The Rev. Abraham Lincoln Washington was arrested for resisting arrest and assaulting a police officer as well as a number of other unfounded charges. Rev. Washington posted bail and was scheduled to come back in one month for the trial. So when his church heard some white teens from the same state were coming to help their church, there was some hesitancy (you can understand why). However, the South Chicago church decided to welcome the youth group. The young Floridians came and had a wonderful week. When they found out what had happened to Rev. Washington, they decided to attend the trial.

The 10 teenagers who had attended the mission trip spread the word, and by the time the trial came, there were 20 students ready to attend. They missed a day of school, drove to the small town, and crowded into the courthouse. Clearly, the policeman and the prosecutor were nervous. The authorities asked the youth worker to leave with his kids because they were making the police officer nervous. Refusing very politely, the youth worker pointed out that he had invited a number of newspapers to cover the story.

The "trial" lasted all day, but the decision took only five minutes: Rev. Washington was acquitted. The young Floridians cheered. Last summer they returned to the South Chicago church, and when they walked in the sanctuary, Rev. Washington interrupted the service and announced, "Here are the

At 19 I received my first paid position in youth ministry. I was attending college and found a part-time position at a church in Compton, California. This was in the late 1960s, just after the Watts riots, so whites were fleeing the community and blacks were moving in. At first glance my new church seemed to be able to live alongside both cultures, and the youth group had students from several ethnic backgrounds. In a few months we grew from six to 50.

Then the senior pastor asked for my resignation. He didn't tell me why. He'd only been there for a few months himself. According to the pastor, the elders made the decision to fire me. I was surprised since most of the elders had children in the youth group, and they seemed pleased with the ministry.

Thirty years later I received a telephone call from this same pastor. He called because his son had attended one of my seminars, and I mentioned that I worked in Compton. This young man asked his dad if he knew me. He did.

Although he had left the Compton church long ago, his son's question brought back some memories and unfinished business, so he called me to explain why I was let go 30 years ago. Apparently, one of the older elders, whose children had already grown up and weren't attending my youth group, told the senior pastor that either I had to go or he had to go. Why? Because I was reaching too many kids from different ethnic backgrounds, and this diversity troubled the elder. The young senior pastor decided I'd have to leave.

But before we got off the phone, my former senior pastor told me something ironic. Less than a year after I was fired, the elder's white daughter married a black man. The elder died three months later of a heart attack.

—*Les Christie*

teenagers who came and supported me during the trial." The entire church rose and gave them a standing ovation.

A group of students from a southern church, where racism was alive and well, experienced the power of diversity and broke down barriers that might never have been broken. Because the youth worker intended to create diversity, he almost lost his job...but he didn't. God was honored because of his courage.

Tribal diversity

Not only is there ethnic diversity in our country, but there is also tribal diversity. Yes, even in our progressive country, we have tribes. In American youth culture, there are many subcultures, and each of these subcultures, or tribes can differ substantially from the others. Tribes are subgroups of adolescents with their own languages, dress codes, music, values, attitudes, and lifestyles. The tribes have many different names: skaters, surfers, skinheads, Goths, kickers, and too many others to include here. Some youth ministries focus on reaching a particular tribe, but again, sameness is still sameness. If a youth ministry reaches skaters but no one from any other tribe attends, everyone is still the same—there is no diversity.

> In many cases, tribes are becoming multiethnic. There used to be a time when we could assume the skaters and bikers would be mostly white whereas hip-hop heads would be mostly black and Hispanic. With movies like *Biker Boys* and *8 Mile*, we see this is no longer true. I never thought I'd see the day when African-American teens would play hockey and go to Marilyn Manson concerts. But I was wrong—that day is upon us!
> —*Efrem Smith*

One woman we know intended to create tribal diversity in her church and youth group. She was an attractive young woman and on the fast track toward a lucrative business career. Deciding, however, that she wanted to delay her career plans to work with inner-city teenagers, she found a position at a church where the mix of people was changing, and, within weeks, she was working with gang members. She successfully convinced a few gang members to attend a Bible study at the church. One night, she was talking about Matthew 6:33, "But seek first his kingdom and his righteousness..." explaining that if a person wants to be a disciple of Jesus, nothing can be more important than Jesus, and she said, "If the gang is more important

> Reconciliation is at work when we go from using language like "those people" to language like "my people." This is the language of the ambassadors of reconciliation—and it should be the language of the church.
>
> —*Efrem Smith*

than Jesus, then the gang has to go. If your girlfriend is more important than Jesus, then the girlfriend has to go." At this, one gang member was so into what she was saying that he reacted violently, throwing his arms back and yelling, "Dude, it's hard to be a disciple!" His elbow crashed through a window. When the church board found out, the members were upset at having to pay $26 to fix the window, so they forbade gang members to use the room. Here was a young woman teaching gang members about Jesus…and they were listening. She was doing such a good job that her kids understood how costly faith is. What a teacher! She had been able to reach a group of students who hadn't been involved in this church before—she was creating tribal diversity. But all the church could think about was broken windows.

It gets worse.

A few weeks later, the pastor accidentally interrupted one of the Bible studies the gang members attended. Invited to sit down, he spent a few minutes talking with the gang members. After he left, one of the guys said, "Hey, I like that guy. Let's go to church this Sunday." When they arrived, the youth worker decided to have the gang members sit in the balcony rather than with the congregation downstairs. While the minister was announcing the giving of the peace, one of the gang members spontaneously stood up and yelled, "Hey, dude, you are cool!" The congregation turned around in shock. After the service the youth worker was told not to bring the gang members back to the church until they learned how to behave in church. If the church had intended to create diversity the way the youth worker had, it would have turned around, invited the gang members downstairs, and applauded a woman who was doing an amazing job of "tribal evangelism." Instead the church fired her. Apparently, this church was more concerned about church decorum than diversity.

Diversity is not always easy, but it's always the right thing to do.

Mental and physical diversity

Because one Lexington, Kentucky, youth group values mental and physical diversity, their ministry has spread. Every year this church sponsors a "Jesus

Prom" for those who never experienced the prom at their high school. The physically and mentally challenged of all ages are invited to the Jesus Prom. Because the prom is planned for a time when tuxedos are in low demand, a local tuxedo shop provides them free of charge, and prom dresses are donated from members in the church who no longer need or wear their prom or evening dresses. Playing the paparazzi, the teens and other members of the church bombard the attendees, taking pictures when each person arrives, reminiscent of the Academy Awards or a new movie premiere. When they arrive at the prom, attendees have hairdressers and manicurists free of charge. Of course there is music, dancing, food, and a photo booth for more formal pictures. This particular church hires limos to transport every person attending from the dinner to the dance, which are held in different buildings on the church property. The Jesus Prom has become a huge event and is now happening nationwide.

You can learn more about hosting the Jesus Prom in your area by contacting Southland Christian Church:

Jesus Prom
Southland Christian Church
P.O. Box 23338
Lexington, KY 40523
859.224.1664
www.southlandchristian.org/classes/specneeds/jesusprom/

What a ministry! The youth group interacts with people of all different ability levels, and everyone benefits. By interacting with students who are usually considered "handicapped," others in the youth group learn more about their own gifts and the many gifts the mentally and physically challenged have to offer, and their diversity is valued.

I'm concerned about how many churches deal with generational diversity. It seems they believe it's more important to relieve the pressure that exists between the old and the young than to heal it. The easiest way, of course, to accomplish this is to splinter the church into generationally distinct congregations—a church service for children, a church service for youth, and several generational-based adult services.

This approach does deal with the immediate problem of tension, but it robs the body of much of its power—the old can no longer be challenged by the brash audacity of the young; and the young can no longer benefit from the experience, wisdom, and stability of the old. By definition the body is diverse, and in 1 Corinthians 12, Paul addresses the problem of segregating the parts. His instructions are that we should work together. I do not suggest that we eliminate age-specific programming in our churches. But we must calculate the cost of intentionally segregating generations simply to make life easier for everyone.

—*Marv Penner*

After more than 25 years of ministry to teenagers, I do have some favorite students. One of my all-time favorites was Adam. Adam had Down's. Adam stood 6 feet 2 inches tall, weighed 220 pounds, and had a smile the size of the Grand Canyon. My favorite memory is when Adam got a job at McDonald's wiping tables. Not knowing Adam was working, I walked in and immediately heard a scream from clear across the room: "Dan Jessup! Dan Jessup! Dan Jessup!" I looked up, and there was Adam, wet rag in hand, running toward me with his arms open wide. Somehow I think Adam's total abandon for his friends and complete disregard for what's "proper" drew me a little closer to the heart of Jesus.

I got to know Adam through Partners, a marvelous ministry in Colorado Springs. For the last 15 years, every Thursday evening, students with all kinds of special needs crowd into a room for an evening of singing, games, and a short talk about Jesus. Blind students, Down's students, wheelchair-bound students, mentally disabled students…it's what I imagine the pool at Bethesda looked like.

One night Frank Early, our Partners staff man who spent most of his life on crutches or in a wheelchair because of cerebral palsy, decided to put on a formal dance for the students. No one ever invites special-needs kids to the local high school homecoming dance, so for the first time ever, these kids went dress and suit shopping. Frank got all kinds of CDs, videos, DVDs, and gift certificates donated, and the students came decked out in their finest apparel. I was DJ and MC, so I was responsible for the raffle prizes. I would call out a gift, pick a kid's name, and the crowd would cheer. It was a hoot!

These students have special needs, but they are not disabled! This ministry understands that diversity is a gift to the teenagers and to everyone one who comes close to it.

—*Dan Jessup*

Generational diversity

Mostly, when we focus on ethnic, tribal, and mental and physical diversity, we focus on creating a diverse group of students. However, there are other ways to create diversity. We can have a diverse staff, too. The church should be the place where we grow old together, so we should work hard to connect our students with the whole church, finding ways to break down the youth ghettos in their separate rooms at the back of the church and connecting the teenagers with all the generations in our churches. When the students graduate from our youth programs, their relationships with adults in the church will keep them connected to the church, and they will have reasons to stay in the church. This generational diversity will create friends and long-lasting commitments.

At 76 years of age, Fanny started an amazing intergenerational ministry in the youth group at her church. She became concerned about the teenagers in her church, so she volunteered to help with the high school youth group. "What would you like to do?" the youth pastor asked.

"I don't know," she said, "God and I will think of something." Fanny wasn't a speaker, she felt too old to play games, and she didn't want to lead Bible studies or counsel at camp. But she had an idea. She asked the youth worker to take pictures of every student in the youth group, put each picture on a flash card, and write some biographical information on the back of each. She memorized the picture and the information on each flash card and stood at the door to the youth room each Sunday night. As the students entered, she welcomed each one by name. At the end of the meeting, Fanny stood at the door again, saying goodbye to each person by name and promising to pray. Over the years the church's students discovered that Fanny had the Bible almost memorized, so they came to her with the questions and struggles of their young lives.

Ten years of youth ministry later, at 86, Fanny suffered three strokes. The prospect of her death distressed the kids in the youth group. They wanted to help her, to tell her how much she meant to them, but they didn't know how. One day after he'd finished reading *Tuesdays with Morrie*, the youth leader had an idea. "Fanny," he told her, "I want to do your funeral."

"I know," she said, "I *want* you to do my funeral—but I'm not dead yet."

"Yes, but I want to do your funeral while you are *alive*, so that you can hear just how much you mean to our youth group and our church." Fanny loved the idea, so the youth group and its leader planned her living funeral.

As you might imagine, young men and women packed the service. Many of them had graduated from college. Some were married with children of their own. Ten years' worth of students shared Fanny stories that night. There were stories about how she never lost her youth, even at 86. No old people's perfume for Fanny—she loved expensive designer perfumes like Estée Lauder's "Beautiful," which was her favorite. After the stories, at the end of the evening, a group of high schoolers gathered mysteriously at the back of the room. The teenagers walked down the aisle, clumped together in order to hide something. When they reached the front, they held up a very large, very expensive bottle of "Beautiful" perfume, which they broke and poured over Fanny's feet, anointing her feet in gratitude for all she had done.

Fanny did die later that year, and the youth worker presided at her funeral. At 86 Fanny had already lost most of her friends, and like most older people, would have had just a few close friends left to attend her funeral had she not created generational diversity at her church. More than 500 people showed up at her funeral to celebrate the impact and power of her life…most of the people who came were from the youth group.

Creating this sort of diversity can have a powerful impact on all involved. It can reach people in ways we never thought possible, and it can keep students grounded in the church even after they leave the youth group.

CORE Reality: Diversity

The Ninevites were not pleasant people. Not only were they pagans, they were varsity pagans—wicked. If a prophet wanted to prophecy hell and damnation, he could go to the city of Nineveh. Jonah was waiting for the day he could tell the Ninevites exactly where they would go. God did call him to prophecy in Nineveh, but God wanted Jonah to prophecy repentance, not damnation. Fortunately for the people of Nineveh, God not only loved the Ninevites, but he also had compassion on them. God told his prophet to hurry over to Nineveh to tell them the good news, but Jonah wasn't very thrilled with the prospect and tried to run away. This didn't work, as we all know, and Jonah preached repentance to the Ninevites. Much to his disappointment, the Ninevites listened and repented, so God did not destroy Nineveh. Woo hoo! Start the dancing. God's forgiveness is for all, even wicked-bad sinners. But Jonah wasn't dancing. He knew God was a gracious God, slow to anger and abounding in love. God's inclusiveness forced him to give up exclusiveness. He knew the diversity of the kingdom of God would mean he would have to deal with his own prejudice, his own hatred, and his own pride, so he pouted.

Don't sulk about diversity. Thank God he includes the excluded. Thank God he is slow to anger. Thank God he is abounding in love. Thank God he seeks diversity. And let the dancing begin!

MANDATE: Youth ministry must challenge teenagers to embrace diversity.

CHAPTER SEVEN

CORE REALITY

SANCTUARY

MATTHEW 11:28-30

JOHN 17:15

1 THESSALONIANS 2:7-8

PSALM 91:1-6

Mike's Story

It was 1964, and my years in youth ministry were just beginning. Along with Jim Green and Wayne Rice, I had been hired to create a new outreach ministry for Youth for Christ in San Diego. YFC clubs had become Bible studies for Christian youth, and they wanted to change. Of course there's nothing wrong with Bible studies for Christians, but YFC was supposed to be a parachurch organization, an outreach to kids who didn't go to church.

One community in which we worked was Point Loma, a small area located on the peninsula between the Pacific Ocean and San Diego Bay. Point Loma High School's YFC club was averaging about eight students a week. After a few weeks of groundwork, spending time on campus, and building relationships, we decided to start the first Campus Life club in the United States, and it was designed specifically for outreach. Our first meeting was held on a Thursday evening in a beautiful mansion-sized house on the San Diego Bay, our board chairman's home.

We had no idea how many kids to expect. We couldn't believe that 150 came! The board chairman was as thrilled as we were. This first meeting was a raucous mix of fun games, loud singing, and a quick, non-churchy talk. One of the games we had was called "First Kiss." Volunteers were taken to another room, and the group was told to say nothing. One volunteer at a time was brought into the room, and I asked them to say something, anything they wanted. The crowd had been told that whatever the volunteers said was what they said right after their first kiss. The first two volunteers said something funny, and they laughed with us. The final volunteer, a varsity football player, was invited into the room. He was not amused, though. After hearing others laugh at what the previous volunteers said, he made up his mind no one would make fun of him. He stubbornly refused to speak. The waiting game continued until, finally, he broke and exclaimed, "S—t!" Of course the crowd exploded in laughter for at least 10 minutes. Unfortunately, one person wasn't laughing—our board chairman.

When the meeting finished, I didn't see either the board chairman or the football player. I searched the house and found them both in an upstairs study where the board chairman had this football player on his knees praying to God. After rescuing the football player, I was lectured by the board chairman: "That word has never been spoken in our home. Not only was it spoken in our home, but it was spoken during a Christian meeting!" Nothing I said made any difference, and the next day our board chairman quit, taking two other members with him.

My ex-board chairman should have quit. He didn't understand the basic tenet of youth ministry: that above all it's a place where students are safe. Our job is not to make non-Christians clean up their language; our job is to treat non-Christians with grace and respect, loving them where they are. As a part of Campus Life, we were not there to treat them as prospective converts to add to our number of people saved or as people who needed to be fixed. Rather part of what we did was to treat them as sheep who needed a shepherd, as hungry who needed food, as thirsty who needed water. This youth ministry, as all youth ministries should be, was to be a sanctuary, a place of worship, safety, and grace where teenagers could be themselves.

It was Friday of Memorial Day weekend. The freeways of Los Angeles were filled with holiday travelers in a hurry to get to their destinations, and traffic was especially heavy on the 405 freeway. Oblivious to a small object on the shoulder just a foot away, thousands of cars rushed by in all four lanes, many going much faster than the 65-miles-per-hour speed limit. It was hard to tell what the small object was: a dead animal, perhaps, or a lost rag doll that had blown out of a car or trailer. No one seemed to care about this object. It was just something else cluttering the L.A. freeways.

Cruising the 405, looking for speeders, a California Highway Patrolman spotted the small object out of the corner of his eye. He didn't think too much about it until he was about to pass and noticed something odd: *it was moving!* Quickly, the officer pulled to the side of the freeway, put on his emergency lights, and ran back to it; he found that the object was not only moving, but it was also very much alive. It was a baby! Unharmed and seemingly unfazed, this little child had somehow crawled onto the freeway without anyone noticing.

When I first read this story (which is true, by the way), my thoughts were of the little baby. Oblivious to the danger, unfazed by the busyness and rush of the traffic, this baby had no idea how close he was to death. I was saddened most by how unprotected this little baby was, exposed to the elements with no place to go and no one to care for him. The babysitter, later arrested for negligence, wasn't caring for him; others didn't notice or thought he wasn't their responsibility. Having wandered away from the sanctuary of his home and the safety of those who loved him, this child needed someone from the outside to provide a sanctuary for him before it was too late.

Could it be that students of this generation are like the baby on the freeway shoulder—in danger, lost, and left to fend for themselves in the busy traffic of our modern culture? Yes, we believe today's teenagers are in peril and desperately need a sanctuary, a refuge, a safe place where they can grow up healthy and whole to face the dangers of modern life. And we believe youth ministry can provide this sanctuary.

Sanctuary is a place of worship.

Because youth programs are for youth, they tend to be filled with activity, noise, busyness, and anxiety. But youth groups should also be a refuge from activity, noise, busyness, and anxiety. A significant part of our youth ministry should be the creation of pockets of silence and solitude where students can reflect, meditate, and contemplate. Many youth groups have game rooms, but few have prayer rooms or quiet rooms where teenagers can pray and be alone with God without interruption. Sometimes our worship is in solitude. Sometimes it is in groups. Youth workers should develop places for students to experience both.

Because worship is more than prayer and song—it is also dancing, creating, reading, writing, journaling, and conversing. A friend of mine in an urban church has created a listening room. People are encouraged to come to this room any time of the night or day and speak to God. They are encour-

---

We tend to think of (and teach) salvation *from* stuff—salvation from sin, from this world, from hell. To the New Testament Jews, however, salvation was more about being saved *to* something. In the same sense, sanctuary isn't just about pulling away *from* the big, bad world; it's more proactive and volitional, a place (and not necessarily a physical place) we *go to*.

—*Mark Oestreicher*

aged to question God, complain to God, or argue with God. When someone goes to the listening room, one of the staff goes into the room and just listens. The listener doesn't respond, answer, or advise the person. He or she just listens, just as God is listening. The listener is there to let the person in the room know that she is not alone, is safe, and is with someone who cares.

We can provide safe places for quiet reflection, and we can create places of sanctuary for worshiping with all of our senses. By providing clay, crayons, construction paper, glue, wood, metal, candles, sand, paints, and incense, we can create a place where students can worship God with their whole bodies and all of their senses. We should encourage them to spend time alone with God, to take a walk or a hike to a secluded place to get in touch with God and with themselves. Worship should not be limited to song; it should be expanded to art, dance, poetry, prose, meditation, and silent prayer. Worship is about experiencing God's presence. How many of us actually include silence, lectio divina (a meditative, prayerful reading of Scripture), journaling, or clay sculpturing in our programs? A sanctuary, a place of worship, provides the means for people to worship in many different ways the God they experience.

Sanctuary is a place of grace.

In the midst of worship, sanctuary is also a place where we experience God's grace. Imagine the chaos that explodes the moment the woman is caught in adultery as described in John 8:

> *There is real hatred in the screaming taunts from the crowd. People rush at this woman, creating a mob scene as they grab stones to kill her. Then Jesus arrives. Sensing an interruption to its murderous rage, the mob begins to quiet down. The pushing and shoving stops, and people move away, creating a space for the woman. She is all alone, in complete silence…and Jesus walks over to her. The fear drains away from her as Jesus comes closer, and the crowd waits in stunned silence. Drawing something in the sand, Jesus says, "If any one of you is without sin, let him be the first to throw a stone at her" (v. 7). He waits while he draws in the sand again. One by one the woman's accusers leave.*

Jesus created sanctuary, a place of grace. He did more than save a woman from being murdered; he eliminated the noise, anxiety, and fear surrounding this woman; he created a space where she could finally see and hear Jesus; and he spoke healing, practical words to her, words she could understand and grasp, words of direction and hope. Like Jesus we should create sanctuary, places of grace, that allow teenagers to take refuge in God's love, where they can experience the forgiveness and presence of God in their lives.

Helen Musick tells the story of a girl in her small group who needed this place of grace. Susan had been a follower of Christ for two years. Prior to her decision to commit to Jesus, she was abused and neglected, and she lived with the pain and guilt of that abuse. However, her encounter with Jesus gave her peace, forgiveness, and joy as she learned what it was to live in the security of a relationship with him. However, over the next two years, the voices of the past seemed to find their way back into her head and heart, causing her to doubt the validity of God in her life and his love for her. Eventually, the voices became too strong: Susan checked herself into a psychiatric hospital hours after she had planned to commit suicide.

Talking with Susan only days after her suicide attempt, Helen was struck by this young woman's assessment of the situation: "Helen, I've been a Christian for two years now. I thought all this crap in my life would be gone, the pain of my past would be eliminated, and I'd be healed."

Helen responded, "Susan, you've been walking with Jesus now for some time, time enough to trust him with the dark holes in your life so that he can breathe healing and life in a way you've never known before. It's taken two years for your healing. Unfortunately, there is much more healing that needs to happen. If I can be blunt, some of the 'crap' of your life is gone, and that is wonderful; there is much more 'crap' to deal with. Luckily, because you are part of the church, we don't have a two-year limit for healing. Your pain is not a sign of God's absence but of God's presence. He has been loving you and healing some of the spaces you have given to him, and now he is asking you to trust him with those other spaces that, until now, have been 'off limits.'"

Susan expected God's grace to run out, his love to give up, and his people to abandon her. She didn't understand that grace is God's eternal sanctuary. As youth workers we need to create places of grace so that students can experience, as Susan did, God's forgiveness, his healing, and his presence— God's grace.

Sanctuary is a place of safety.

When people experience God's grace, they feel safe, so if we create sanctuary in our youth groups, we create an atmosphere of physical, spiritual, and emotional safety. This means that people feel comfortable telling the truth. They don't hold back because they don't have to worry about how what they say will be accepted.

Don't confuse safety with comfort, though, because sanctuary is not a static place, it's a place of action—of active worship, active grace, and active waiting. One of the most effective elements of safety is waiting. Youth ministry is often seen as a place where teenagers get fixed, inoculated from evil, and equipped to face and conquer whatever obstacles may come along. We don't dispute such lofty expectations, but we are realistic, too. Because the world is complicated, youth ministry is about waiting more than fixing. It is about watering and cultivating more than harvesting. I wish someone told me that waiting and patience were the keys to ministry when I started youth work. I had been told that youth ministry is "winning the right to be heard," and this is true—I just didn't realize how long winning that right takes. We wait for our students for as long as they need, so when they are ready, they have a safe place to learn what trusting in God means.

When I was in high school, I found out what it means to have a place

---

I've just worked through another tragic story of a youth worker who crossed the line of moral appropriateness in his relationship with one of the students in his group. These situations are all too common in our churches.

I pose a challenge and a plea to youth workers who know they are vulnerable in some of these areas. If you know that you pose a danger to your students because of issues in your life, I encourage you (beg you!) to step out of ministry voluntarily for a period of time—your reasons don't have to be publicly specific—and get help.

Some of us know that we are not safe with adolescents. Just as it would be inappropriate for an alcoholic to get a job as a bartender, it's inappropriate for some of us to work closely with students. If this is you, please consider quietly stepping aside and letting God heal you before the damage is done.

—Marv Penner

of safety. In my senior year I was actively involved in my youth group. Toward the end of my senior year, I went to the prom…and promptly got drunk. My parents had no idea, but my youth worker heard about it. Confronting me, he expressed his disappointment *as well as* his belief in me. He carefully explained the consequences my action would have on others, but he also explained the consequences of a God who refuses to give up on me. The youth worker was concerned about my failure, yes. But he was also concerned I would believe my failure made me ineligible for grace, and I would no longer be welcome in church. He assured me that I was safe to continue in the youth group, safe to continue my journey with Christ, even though I had lost my way for a while.

Sanctuary is a place of rest.

> *Come to me, all you who are weary and burdened, and I will give you rest. Take my yoke upon you and learn from me, for I am gentle and humble in heart, and you will find rest for your souls. For my yoke is easy and my burden is light.*
>
> (Matthew 11:28-30)

Rest is what we all need but rarely do. It is much easier to rest when we are in a safe place. We have moved way beyond busyness, and those of us in youth ministry know one of the most serious issues facing this generation is stress.

Often for students the demands on their time push them almost beyond their ability to cope. Many students in our youth groups, although apparently happy with their busyness, are actually crumbling under the weight of their schedules, and what they need is rest. Teenagers may respond to a program with a lot of activities and events, but these may actually add to their anxiety and exhaustion rather than relieve it. Part of our responsibility as youth workers is to step into the busyness of our students and say, "Enough is enough. You're doing too much. Quit doing all that you're doing. Slow down. Lighten up. Rest!"

Youth ministry calls students to love Jesus, to follow him. And it calls them to take a nap with him, rest with him, slow down with him, reduce anxiety with him. We provide activities, and we provide a sanctuary from

During a typical day at summer camp, we pack in two chapel sessions, cabin time, night games, free time, meals, massive water balloon fights, and more. Tucked into the middle of the craziness is what we call "H2" or "horizontal hour." It falls immediately after lunch and before four hours of chaotic free time. At the beginning of the week, kids buck at the requirements of H2—they must be horizontal on their beds, quiet, and in rest mode for a full hour. But by Wednesday afternoon, counselors have to shake campers from a deep sleep so they're not late for skeet shooting! Not only does God ask us to be still, but we also *need* to be still. As youth workers we should help teenagers discover that need.

—*Heather Flies*

activity. Our job is to bring teenagers into activity so they can find Jesus, so they can find their souls *and* find *rest* for their souls.

Sanctuary is a place of growth.

When we provide a place of worship, grace, safety, and rest, we also provide a place for kids to grow. Psalm 91 makes it clear that sanctuary is a place of growth, for being nurtured, mothered, and protected. A sanctuary becomes a place where we can regain our strength, get our bearings, heal our wounds, and lose our fears—places of maturation and discipleship. However, youth groups do not exist to pamper students or to create a spiritual Disneyland so

Sanctuary doesn't mean youth group should always be a comfortable place, but it will be a place where those who are uncomfortable are welcome with open arms of grace. Too often the church is like a hospital that makes the sick feel unwelcome and allows the healthy to develop habits that will make them sick.

Youth ministries that create sanctuary will be places that welcome the unhealthy but do whatever is necessary to bring about—to grow—health and wholeness.

—*Duffy Robbins*

they never have to interact with the world. We provide a sanctuary so our students can be in the world but not of it. Youth ministry does have boundaries; it does nudge teenagers out of the nest when they are strong enough to fly.

Nudging, sometimes pushing, out of the nest means requiring students to be responsible for their actions and for their lives. In one youth group, just as one of its members was to be pushed out of the nest, to be taught responsibility, the others in the group balked. This one member made a bad decision and was in trouble, and the youth group wanted to help her by sending other youth groups in the area the following letter:

> *We're members of a youth group a lot like yours. We meet every week for Bible study and fun. We're friends at school, we're learning about what it means to be the Church—to be Christians no matter where we are...*
>
> *Anyway, we're writing to tell you about one of our friends, Tessy, who needs our help and yours. Tessy is a member of our youth group. She's on the cross-country team at school, on the track team, in the a capella group, and she's a good student. Everybody likes her. However, she did a really stupid thing not too long ago! Tessy took her parents' car without permission and wrecked it. She's okay, but there is almost $2,300 in damage to the car. Tessy has her permit, but not her driver's license, so insurance won't pay for the damage. Tessy feels really bad, and she's never done anything like this before. But her parents are making her pay for the whole thing, and now she has to quit sports to get a job, and she probably won't be able to go on any of the choir trips. Work is hard to find here, but she's looking, and even when she finds a job, it will take forever to pay off the $2,300. Her whole year is ruined, and she may not even get it paid off before next year when she'll be a senior. We feel bad for her! Will you help us help her? We're writing every youth group we can think of asking two things. One, will you write Tessy and tell her that even though you don't know her you feel bad for her? And two, could you take up a little collection to help Tessy pay for her huge debt? If you could each just share 50 cents or a dollar it would help pay for the car and make Tessy feel better about herself. We're not asking you to send a lot of money, but we're asking lots of groups to send a little. Wouldn't you want someone to help you out?*

Tessy stole her parents' car, driving it without a legal license or insurance, and the youth group wanted to help by eliminating the consequences. Ridiculous! The letter and the assistance the youth group asks for are not ways to help Tessy. This isn't grace; it's not safety. It is enabling. The youth leaders should never have allowed this letter to be sent because it stunts the growth of this young girl. Tessy needed to learn responsibility and consequence by paying for the repairs herself. This youth group did not provide sanctuary. Sanctuary does not rescue or remove consequences. Sanctuary does not help people escape punishment; rather it is with them through the punishment.

If youth ministry provides sanctuary, then we must provide a place where teenagers grow. If the youth group had helped Tessy find a job and encouraged her to share her story with others so they might not make the same bad decision, then it would be providing sanctuary. Instead of bailing her out, they could have said, "Even though you have to quit choir and your 'whole year is ruined,' Tessy, we will support you and cheer you up when the days get tough." They could have promised to bring her videos and pictures of the choir tour. They could even have sent a letter to Tessy's parents, committing themselves to helping her keep her commitment. By being with her through the consequences of her "stupid" decision, the youth group could have helped Tessy to grow. Nothing could be more important and helpful than a place where there is support and encouragement to grow— a sanctuary.

CORE Reality: Sanctuary

Recently, a youth worker from a church in San Francisco wrote to the folks at DCLA, asking for a scholarship for one of her kids. Without realizing it, Jen Arens, the youth pastor, by describing her youth group, gave a working definition of the CORE reality of sanctuary:

I go to the coolest church. With an average of about 75 people on a Sunday, we are made up of more than 25 nationalities and 14 native languages. We are the church with its sleeves rolled up, where the recovering sits next to the reformed prostitute and where the sweetest old lady has no problem hugging the smelliest old homeless guy. And, man, does my church love kids.

At least monthly my kids are asked to dance a hula or hip-hop during worship. Youth is celebrated in our church. We never get threatened with the fires of hell when things get destroyed; they just fix it. No one cares that the youth worker's office looks like chaos vomited or that the teens used the chapel for a WWF Smackdown fight. My church could care a flying rip when we break a window during a marathon session of warball; they just love the kids like Jesus would.

Unfortunately, to get to my church you have to walk through dirty, urine-stenched streets; step over a drunken man passed out in our doorway, and avoid the dealers on the corner as you risk being propositioned by four or five transgender prostitutes. Basically, to get to my church, you have to sift through the garbage left by life, garbage my youth live in every day.

For the most part the kids in my youth group live in one-bedroom or studio apartments with four or five other people. They are the kids whose parents work too much, or are addicted too much, or just don't care enough to even come home at night. Some of my kids have never even slept in a real bed. Before I became the youth worker, most of my teenagers had never eaten in a restaurant, gone to the movies or even been to the beach, which is less than two miles away.

I am fortunate enough to have 25 percent of my church budget dedicated to youth programs. That may seem pretty astounding, but you need to remember that my congregation is made up of recovering addicts, reformed prostitutes, and homeless men and women. Our budget is minute. For my kids to go to any kind of an event, our church has to pay everything: registration, housing, gas, and food. Our kids don't have any money, our church doesn't have much, and our community isn't very fundraising friendly. But thank God for my church that welcomes all kids and provides them a sanctuary in the middle of the city.

MANDATE: Youth ministry must provide a safe place for students.

CHAPTER EIGHT

CORE REALITY

INTIMACY

JOHN 13:34-35; 15:1-17

MARK 14:3-9

REVELATION 2:4-5

Mike's Story

Intimacy is not easy for me. In fact, I was 50 years old before I received my first glimpse of intimacy with God. I have written often about my experience at L'Arche, a community of mentally and physically challenged adults, because it was a defining moment in my relationship with God; it was the moment I first noticed Jesus. Although I thought he was a long way away from me, unhappy with me, frustrated because I wasn't doing better in my walk with him, Jesus had been with me, right next to me all my life. I just hadn't noticed him.

Shortly after my experience at L'Arche, I read Brennan Manning's *Lion and Lamb: The Relentless Tenderness of Jesus.* He referred to the way Jesus stalks us, and I remember thinking, "What?!? Jesus is not stalking me! He's mad at me; he's disgusted with me; he doesn't like me! Oh, yeah, he's stalking me all right; he can hardly wait to get his hands on me and send me straight to hell!" I honestly believed I didn't have Jesus' approval, and Brennan was writing to and about people like me: those of us who don't want Jesus around because we're afraid of his disapproval.

Fortunately, Brennan also writes about the Shepherd's response: "I will not leave you alone. You are Mine. I know each of my sheep by name. You belong to Me. If you think I am finished with you, if you think I am a small god that you can keep at a safe distance, I will pounce upon you like a roaring lion, tear you to pieces, rip you to shreds, and break every bone in your body. Then I will mend you, cradle you in My arms, and kiss you tenderly" (Chosen Books, 1986. p. 129). Brennan was telling me that Jesus wanted to get his hands on me—but only so he could cradle me, not condemn me.

It's been a decade since my introduction to the tender Jesus, the one who wants to be next to me, and I wish I could say the battle's over, that I know beyond a shadow of doubt Jesus just wants to be next to me, but I still doubt, still have my bad days. In preparation for this book, I came across a journal entry I made. On that day I decided to write a letter from Jesus:

Michael…Michael…
You know, don't you? Your mind knows more than your heart can grasp. You
are so outgoing, so willing to talk publicly about me, and so afraid to be
alone with me. You know I have scarred your soul, don't you? You know I
have claimed you as my own, don't you? My claim supercedes all other
claims, but I can still feel your reluctance, your resistance, your fear, your
anxiety that my love is conditional, weak, fragile, tenuous. I have the feel-
ing your trust of my love will be a lifetime project. But you know I know
now. You know that even your unbelief draws me to you, makes me love
you more. I will just sit here and wait until your knowledge of my love
seeps into the cracks and crevices of the dark and hidden parts of your
soul where you can finally fall asleep in my arms.

—Jesus

Intimacy is a lifelong journey, and it is a journey worth taking. Now I look back to when I started youth ministry 42 years ago and understand that I was arrogant, cocky, confident, and willing to gamble it all on Jesus. And I realize Jesus was there, too. He was there in my arrogance, my cockiness, and my confidence. He was pushing me to gamble it all on him, pushing me to do more; he was the one encouraging me not to worry about failure or criticism; he was the one driving me to break boundaries, to rebel against the system. Perhaps Jesus remembered his early days, when he disobeyed his parents and went to the temple because he was passionate about his calling, anxious to get started, and eager to take on the system. Jesus was the one whispering to me, "You crack me up, Michael; you are just crazy enough and wild enough and irresponsible enough to be my disciple. I am so proud of you." I couldn't hear it then, but I hear it now—every night when I fall asleep and every morning when I wake up.

Our relationships with Jesus are where our youth ministries begin and end. Because we cannot separate our personal ministries about Jesus from our personal relationships with Jesus, *our first priority in ministry is intimacy with God, not lessons about God.* Fruitful ministry is not the result of our dynamic programs, our gifts, or our theological and doctrinal dexterity; it is the consequence of being with Jesus. Our devotion to Jesus is the cornerstone of our ministries because he's the cornerstone of life. Paul said we are all members of God's household with "Christ Jesus himself as the chief cornerstone. In him the whole building is joined together and rises to become a holy temple in the Lord" (Ephesians 2:20-21).

Jesus is the cornerstone of our ministries; Jesus is the building block that supports us; Jesus holds us together; Jesus transforms and unites ordinary youth workers into a holy temple. Wow! For this transformation to take place, though, we must be intimate with Jesus, get to know him, and let him know us. Here are seven ministry-altering insights about intimacy with Jesus. They'll alter your life, too.

1. My soul is more important than my student's soul.

Aren't all souls equal to God? Certainly, as far as God is concerned. As far as each one of us is concerned, though, our individual relationships with God are primary because we are responsible for our own response to God. God desires a relationship with me, he calls my name, and I am the only one who can answer that call.

Many people will agree that their relationships with God are primary, but if they kept a record of time they spent on their relationships with God compared to time they spent on the students' relationships with God, it would tell a different story. It might tell us that although we can agree at the intellectual level, most youth workers, in terms of energy, time, and commitment, don't agree at the practical level—they don't *live* like their souls are more important than their students' souls. When we become eager to tear Satan's worldly grasp from our kids' hearts, we don't remember to pluck the world out of our own hearts first, and we can't minister effectively when our hearts and souls are focused on this world rather than God.

In fact, many of us take our souls for granted. We assume we have an intimate relationship with Jesus because we believe in Jesus; we confuse belief with relationship, and we substitute our initial commitment and acceptance of Christ for our daily, continual conversation with Christ. Our initial decision to follow Jesus is, we think, transformed into our daily relationship with him. Our thoughts often go something like this: "I became a Christian, I go to church, I read my Bible periodically, and I'm doing godly work. Therefore, I have a relationship with Jesus." When we think like this, our conversion becomes the defining focus of our relationship with Jesus. This is

Silence. It's one of God's greatest gifts to us but one of the hardest to appropriate. I took my first silent retreat last year. It took me only 20 years of ministry to discover that silence was the place I would meet God most intimately, the place where my relationship with him would grow. Busyness and noise have become the greatest enemies of my closeness with God, of my journey with God.

I always believed prayer meant talking. I'm not sure where I learned that, but I think it was in church. I have learned now, though, that prayer is communicating, and some of the deepest communication is nonverbal.

—*Helen Musick*

like a couple whose marriage ceremony becomes the defining moment of their relationship: the rest of the marriage is pretty weak. The marriage ceremony is important; it is the *beginning*, the start, the inauguration of a lifetime spent relating to each other, but it is only the start. Our commitment to Jesus launches us into a journey, into a lifetime relationship with him.

Peter got stuck on his initial commitment to follow Christ. He thought he had it figured out, that his first commitment was all he needed. However, when we read the story of Peter, we are bewildered by how much of his relationship with Jesus he still doesn't understand. Even though we know better, we still think, "What happened to Peter would never happen to me. I won't turn from Jesus." Peter was convinced it wouldn't happen to him, either. He believed he was totally committed to Jesus and more dedicated than anyone else. He thought he understood exactly who Jesus was, who he was, and what he could do. But Jesus knew better.

He knew that Peter had much to learn and a long way to grow—just as we do—and here's what's crazy: Jesus warned Peter. He tried to prepare Peter, but Peter wasn't listening. He wasn't spending time in relationship with Jesus. He was listening to the excitement of following Jesus, the exhilaration of watching people healed, critics silenced, lives changed, and miracles accomplished. Fortunately, Peter finally figured it out, but not before his lack of intimacy was exposed the night he denied Christ.

Earlier, in John 21, Jesus questions Peter, over and over again: "Do you truly love me more than these?" In every instance Peter's answer to this question precedes Jesus' command, "Feed my sheep." Jesus questions us, too, and our answers must come before his command. Our relationships with Jesus must precede our ministries with students.

2. Time alone with Jesus is more important than time alone with students.

It sounds scandalous, self-centered, and selfish to suggest that our time alone with Jesus is more important than time alone with students, but if we are responsible for our own souls first, time with God is important. Jesus himself is an example of the need to spend time alone with God. First he waited almost 30 years, time spent growing with God, before he was ready to fulfill his ministry. Then throughout his three years of ministry, Jesus continually went somewhere by himself to pray and spend time with his father, leaving his disciples alone. In fact, Luke tells us that Jesus often withdrew to lonely places and prayed (5:16). Also, when the disciples were overwhelmed by the

> As an extreme extrovert I have a hard time nurturing my soul in quiet time alone with God, but I know I need to. It was that knowledge that led me to schedule a 48-hour retreat of solitude at a hermitage an hour north of my home. As the time approached for me to walk into that intimate time with the Lord, my cell phone and e-mail account were overloaded with messages from students and parents: Kelsey was thinking about suicide again; Jake was caught looking at porn online; the Johnson family was moving to Texas. I needed to minister to these people.
>
> As I was planning how I would explain to the caretakers at the hermitage why I needed to cancel, I sensed God gently and repeatedly whispering, "What about you and me?" So I went on my retreat, and those 48 hours were life-changing. And it was better for Kelsey, Jake, and the Johnsons, too, because later that week they received ministry from a woman who'd just spent 48 hours alone with God.
>
> —Heather Flies

crowds who were just discovering their Savior, Jesus said to them, "Come with me by yourselves to a quiet place and get some rest" (Mark 6:31).

If even the son of God, the Messiah, realized the importance of spending time in relationship with God, then there is no way we can minister without spending time with God. Jesus is in control of the souls of our students; we are not. *There is only one Messiah, and you aren't it.* Jesus refused to be ruled by the urgent needs of the masses. Instead he was ruled by his desire to stay close to his father. This is not scandalous; this is relationship. The real scandal of youth ministry is how little time alone with Jesus those in youth ministry actually spend!

3. Friendship is more important than discipleship.

How can friendship be more important than discipleship? Well, the desire to follow God arises from the desire to spend time alone with God, learning more about and befriending him. What makes the incarnation radical is that God's love for us is expressed in his desire to become *one of us*, and Jesus defined this love as friendship: "Greater love has no one than this, that he lay down his life for his friends" (John 15:13). By laying down his life for us, Jesus is saying that he is, first and foremost, our friend; he makes disciples one friend at a time. Our discipleship springs from his radical act of friendship. Too many of us choose discipleship (doing) over friendship (being) and, as a result, lose ourselves in activity instead of intimacy. God loves us, and that is important, but more importantly, he likes us. He really, really likes us! He even wants to hang out with us.

In *The Signature of Jesus*, Brennan Manning tells the story of a woman who recognized her friendship with Christ during a retreat he was leading for a group of nuns. When the group arrived one morning, one of the nuns was noticeably excited.

"Father Manning," Sister Catherine blurted out, "I had the most amazing dream last night. Would you like to hear about it?"

"Of course." What else could he say?

"Well, I dreamed I was at a school dance. Everyone at the dance had made a circle around the dance floor so they could choose a partner and dance to the first song. By the time everyone was done choosing, I was the only one standing alone. No one had chosen me. Feeling rejected and alone I looked up to see a strikingly handsome young man enter the room. From the moment he entered the room, his eyes were fixated on mine. Determined, he walked straight toward me, crossing the middle of the dance floor. As he passed each couple, they stopped and watched as he walked up to me and asked me to dance. My heart was beating wildly. I was swept into his arms,

---

Friendship is the best outcome that discipleship can ever achieve. The next time you're with your key leaders, try to begin the process toward friendships with them by just talking about life. Talk about everyday, trivial things that you love, like, don't like, or can't stand; talk about things that worry you or make you laugh. It's a great way to keep from compartmentalizing the relationship between youth worker and key leaders into a ministry-only box.

—Fred Lynch

and we began to dance with abandon across the floor. As we danced I couldn't help but notice his hands; they were scarred as though someone had driven nails through his hands. Just as I was beginning to recognize this man, he suddenly leaned over, put his lips right next to my ear, and whispered, 'Catherine, I'm crazy about you.'" Everyone in the Bible study, including Brennan, was moved to tears. (Chosen Books, 1988. p. 174)

Jesus is our friend, cheering us on, cherishing us, filled with affection and pride, anxious to remind us, "I'm crazy about you." It could just be that the most important part of our youth ministries is our friendship with Jesus. Maybe by seeing our friendship with Jesus, those around us will want to be friends with Jesus, too.

4. Eternity is more important than time.

As our friendship with Jesus develops, we will spend time listening to him, learning what is important to him. In *A Testament of Devotion*, Thomas Kelly describes this: "Deep within us all there is an amazing inner sanctuary of the soul, a holy place, a Divine Center, a *speaking voice*, to which we may continually return" (HarperCollins, 1941. p. 9). He warns, though, that this secret place of the soul can become a "noisy workshop." Kelly also writes about the "mysterious *many-ing* of God" (p. 10), a great phrase he invented. One instance of this "many-ing of God" is described in Acts 2: the Holy Spirit explodes into the world, and people are converted left and right. One of the reasons we are in youth ministry is to aid in the "many-ing" of the kingdom of God, which occurs when God, who is eternal, enters our lives in time. We are anxious to see the many-ing of God, to see students transformed by the good news of the gospel.

However, Kelly explains there is also a "one-ing" of those souls who find their way back to God (p. 47), who come home to God. We are concerned not only with God's entry into our world of time and space, but also with our return to him in eternity. This is the "Divine Center" Kelly describes. This is where we can listen to the "speaking voice" as long as we don't clutter it with the noise of this world. So before we see the many-ing of our ministry in this world, we need to see the one-ing of our relationship with God in eternity.

In this world, time is short. We are told we need to redeem time, to manage our time efficiently and carefully. But Christians don't take time seri-

Intimacy is born out of chaos—even the wild unpredictability of life. That's when I have experienced some of my best soul-searching and life-defining interactions—when my world gets turned upside down. Most importantly, chaos deepens my intimacy with God. I pray more, listen more. My mess drives me to my knees. The intensity of life can get so overwhelming that I have nowhere else to go but to the One who operates outside and within the perceived confusion, the One who's in eternity and has entered this world. And here is what I have learned about prayer: *Prayer doesn't reduce the chaos; it increases my faith.* I trust Jesus even more. Intimacy is born out of the bedlam that is my life!

—Charley Scandlyn

ously. *We take eternity seriously.* We believe in a God who is not limited by time. Time is subject to God, and God works whenever he wants, however he wants. We trust that God is working even when we can't see or feel it. Therefore, youth workers should refuse to become frantic and frenzied, filling their lives with cluttered calendars and busy schedules, cramming into every second another activity. Instead we should choose to live an unhurried life where time is not a tyrant, trusting that God is present in time and in eternity. Then we can relax, resting in his agenda, not ours.

Kelly goes on to describe what our lives will be like when we listen to the "speaking voice" deep within us, reminding us that we are not subject to time, but our time is subject to God's eternity: "Life from the center is a life of unhurried peace and power. It is simple. It is serene. It is amazing. It is triumphant. It is radiant. It takes no time, but it occupies all our time. And it makes our life programs new and overcoming. We need not get frantic. He is at the helm. And when our little day is done, we lie down quietly in peace, for all is well" (p. 78).

5. My security is in God, not my ministry.

Youth ministry is a powerful platform. Influencing and shaping teenagers' lives is a wonderful calling—and a dangerous one. It is dangerous because students can put youth workers on pedestals or become dependent on them. For us the issue is not so much about the students' dependence or idolization, but it is really about how we as youth workers respond to it. Unless we're careful, we can begin to depend on the youth for our self-worth. If the kids like us, if our numbers are growing, if the kids express how much we help them, and if parents are supportive—then we feel good about our ministries. But if our programs are not growing, if kids don't respond, and if parents question us—then we don't feel good about our ministries. And if our self-worth is tied to our ministries, then we don't feel good about ourselves; we feel worthless. When we're insecure about our ministries and ourselves, we can easily project our lack of security onto the youth group. What happens then? We become anxious, manipulative, and pushy. We compensate for our own feelings of inadequacy by seeking affirmation for and success in our programs.

But what does intimacy with Jesus have to do with our insecurity? *Everything!* Read Mark 10:13-16 and imagine how the children must have felt when the disciples reprimanded them for trying to get close to Jesus. Now imagine how they must have felt when Jesus reprimanded the disciples instead and asked the children to come to him. Mark tells us that when the children came to him, "he took the children in his arms, put his hands on them and blessed them." When you and I are held in the arms of Jesus, when we have been touched and blessed by the Savior, when we have been called "beloved," our insecurity disappears. Our individual, intimate relationships with Jesus are what keep our blessedness in the center of our lives. Some may tell us we don't have enough students, we don't have enough activities, we don't attract the right kind of teenagers, or we don't get big enough results. Others may tell us we're too old, we're too young, we're not gifted enough, or we're not cool enough. But when you and I have been held in the arms of Jesus, and he has blessed us and laid his hands on us, then nothing can stop us from the youth ministry God has called us to do.

6. The heart is more important than the head.

In their book, *The Sacred Romance*, Brent Curtis and John Eldredge state unequivocally, "The Christian life is a love affair of the heart." Our security in Christ is not based on rational explanations; it is based on his presence in

I get a little uncomfortable when we make a dichotomy between the head and the heart. Any youth worker who's had to deal with what I call "retreat reentry syndrome" can't help but wonder which will last longer in his kids—the poison ivy, the mosquito bites, or the heartfelt rededication commitment made on that last night.

Experience soon teaches us that real-life discipleship takes more than warm fuzzies and neat memories. The fuel for long-term Christian commitment is God's truth—not goose bumps. Our students need heartfelt spiritual experiences as well as intellectual spiritual content: soul, heart, *and* mind.

—*Duffy Robbins*

our hearts. Jesus' summary of the law is clear, "Love the Lord your God *with all your heart...*" (Matthew 22:37, Mark 12:30, Luke 10:27). Principles, ethics, programs, doctrines, and theology are important, but as Curtis and Eldredge note, "What God cares about is the inner life, the life of the heart." We agree. The heart is the home of our passions, our "center," the wellspring of our souls. However much we might agree with this in theory, in practice it is often different. The problem many of us in ministry have is the same problem the people of David's city had when Isaiah prophesied, "The Lord says: 'These people...honor me with their lips, but their hearts are far from me'" (29:13). We are excellent with our lips, but it's our hearts we need to worry about. It's our souls we need to tend. It's the closeness of our hearts to Jesus' heart that is the issue.

We are not anti-thinking, nor are we anti-intellect. We *are* pro-heart. Our hope and prayer is that every youth worker will commit to loving God completely: mind, soul, *and* heart.

7. The "silent skills" are more effective than the "noisy skills."

When God touches our hearts, when we commit them to Jesus, we learn more about ministry from him than seemed possible. He shows us what "silent skills" are; he models them for us. In our ministries we should learn to use these "silent skills" more frequently than the "noisy" ones.

> Admittedly, I'm one who tends to trust more in the noisy than the silent skills. Because of this, I look for ministry models who rely on the silent skills—and my search led me to Greg. Greg has quietly and faithfully ministered to students for 18 years. He doesn't listen to the hip-hop station. His favorite movie is *The Sound of Music*. And he thinks "Gap" refers to a dental problem. But Greg comes alongside students—listening, noticing, and praying. I want to be like Greg.
>
> —*Heather Flies*

Before we go any further, though, we should define them. Noisy skills are the external skills, the ones we can see: programming skills, speaking skills, administrative skills, large-group leadership skills, and small-group leadership skills. Noisy skills can be good; they are powerful and effective. There is nothing wrong with getting students to your meetings, making teenagers laugh, keeping them interested during Bible studies, making an event happen, or directing games and Bible studies. But intimacy with Jesus produces different skills—"silent skills." These skills include our abilities to listen, notice, intuit, and empathize—the skills of the heart. These skills don't make the headlines, but they are the skills we develop when we are intimate with Jesus, and they are critical to our ministry with students.

Listening. The adolescent world is a world of noise. They are continually barraged with sounds. When they come to youth group, they should experience something different: the power of quiet. Very few people listen to adolescents, but youth workers do. Because an intimate relationship with Jesus is one of silence and listening, we become adept at listening to others when we are intimate with him. Taking the time to listen to a student, disciplining ourselves to hear what he or she is saying verbally and nonverbally, powerfully communicates how much we care for that young person. Listening to a student's body language is much more important than listening to his or her words.

Noticing. Noticing means we pay attention. Noticing may not seem very important, but it is one of the most neglected life skills. When we care for someone, we notice what others don't notice. We notice when the person we care about is in a bad mood, upset, mad, sick, lonely, hurt, preoccupied, or depressed. People who don't care about us don't notice the clues we give about what's going on in our hearts. Youth workers should be known as *noticers*. We care about our kids and pay attention to them—we watch them carefully; we recognize when life is not going well; and we respond when no one else responds. When we care about teenagers, we pay attention to them. Noticing the intricacies of our students' lives shouts to them, *"You matter."*

Intuiting. Intuition is a spooky skill. Not everyone has it, and those who do must be very careful and use it sparingly. Intuition is a kind of instinct, a premonition, or perception; it is a knowing that comes from a long connection with a person or group. If you have watched couples who've been married for a long time, you have seen intuition. Each one seems to know what the other is going to do before it's done. When you and I care deeply about our kids and get to know them, often we can sense trouble before it happens; we can sense that a particular student is about to explode or break down. Logically, there might be no concrete reason for why we think he or she is about to break down, but because we know the kid, we just know something's up—we intuit it.

Empathizing. Empathy is the ability to suffer with someone who is suffering and experience joy with someone who is happy. Empathy is the ability to get inside other people's emotions and feel what they feel. It is the ability to identify with others, to show understanding and compassion. When suffering, pain, fear, and doubt distance and isolate our students from us, empathy closes the distance and connects us with them.

When we allow Jesus to be intimate with us, he listens, notices, intuits, and empathizes. We know, then, that Jesus cares for and about us. If we can learn these "silent skills" from Jesus, we can begin to develop relationships with our students. Then they might just catch a glimpse of what intimacy with Christ is like and seek it for themselves.

CORE Reality: Intimacy

A number of years ago Amy Grant received an award from Saint John's Abbey and University in St. Cloud, Minnesota. The Pax Christi Award honors unusual expressions of Christian faith and values. When Amy came forward to receive the award, she told the following story:

I had three nieces who, by the time they were almost in high school, had never seen the ocean. I was lucky enough to take them to the beach for the first time, with their moms. We got there right at the end of the day, and the sun was shining so bright. I made them not peek across the highway because the ocean's on one side and all the places people stay are on the other.

And I said, "Wait, let's go drop our bags, put on the clothes that we're going to dinner in, and on the way to the restaurant, let's go to the beach." We drove and parked in the parking lot on the opposite side of the highway. I said, "Close your eyes. You're not going to believe this. Close your eyes."

That's an old wooden bridge that's about two-and-a-half stories high that crosses the highway. My heart was pounding that I got to be the lucky one to make this introduction.

And with eyes closed, they're climbing those stairs and walking across the top of that bridge. You could hear the highway under them, but it's nothing compared to the roar of that sea.

When I got to the top of that bridge, I said, "Open your eyes!"

And they saw that water and started laughing and screaming, because you know what? Postcards don't do the ocean justice. TV and surround-sound, they don't come close. The next thing I knew, those girls were running down the other side of those steps, straight into the water with their dinner clothes on.

I think the love of God is like the ocean. It's the greatest component of our world even though we don't see it a lot of the time.

What an honor for me to get to introduce so many people to such a grand thing.

(*Campus Life*, July/August 1994. p. 22)

We agree. To share the reckless, wild, roaring love of God with students is a very grand thing indeed. And an even grander thing is to be intimate with it, to experience it firsthand, to soak in it—clothes and all.

MANDATE: Our relationship with Jesus is our youth ministry.

CHAPTER NINE

CORE REALITY

MYSTERY

1 CORINTHIANS 13:12

ISAIAH 55:8-9

JOB 11:7-9

ECCLESIASTES 11:5

Mike's Story

It was my first year of youth ministry. I brought a group of high school students to Hume Lake Conference Center in central California for a weeklong summer camp. One of the high school students had quite a story. At 17 he already had a long history of drugs and violence. A few months before camp, on a drug-induced high, he drove his car at 100 miles per hour through a red light and plowed into another car. Miraculously, the people in the other car were not seriously hurt, but Jerry came very close to dying. During his lengthy recovery he decided the accident was a wake-up call, and he thought attending church would be a good first step in cleaning up his life.

I was only a couple of years older than he was and, frankly, very insecure about whether, as his counselor, I could handle him. I was new to youth work and was still a bit immature myself. And I had never been a camp counselor before. There were still a lot of things about youth ministry I did not know. I also did not know that, back at my home church, a group of adults was praying every night for Jerry to become a Christian.

Nothing happened during the first three days; Jerry seemed totally unresponsive at the evening campfires. On the fourth night he told me that he wasn't going to campfire; he and his best friend, Dan, were ditching the meeting. Because I was immature and insecure, I wanted Jerry to like me, so I told him that I would ditch the meeting with him and Dan. We decided to hide in the prayer chapel—no one would think to look for us there.

Of course we were missed, and the adult leaders scoured the grounds searching for us, and of course they never looked in the prayer chapel. While the evening meeting was being held, we started talking about guy things: girls, sports, girls, a little about life, girls. Jerry was the worldly-wise one, so he kept our attention as he talked about his life of sex, drugs, and rock and roll. Dan and I were on the edge of our seats, rapt with attention. In the middle of the conversation, Jerry suddenly quit talking.

He was silent for a few minutes. Then he said to us, "I can't believe you guys came up here with me even though we're all going to get in trouble, especially you because you're church people." He paused..."So what is the Christianity thing, anyway?" Dan and I looked at each other in shock and began to stumble over our words, trying to tell Jerry about Jesus. When we finished, Jerry was silent again. Then he looked up and said, "Okay, guys, you know my story. I'm a very messed-up guy, but what you said about Jesus makes sense to me. So what do I have to do to become a Christian?" Again we were dumfounded. Once we caught our breath, we led Jerry in a prayer to invite Jesus Christ into his life.

When we walked out of the prayer room, we could hardly wait to tell the leaders what happened. They, of course, could hardly wait to tell us what was going to happen to us. That night God surprised us all. He had honored Jerry and his Christian friend's stubborn refusal to attend the campfire as well as my immaturity to go with them. He transformed our rule breaking into a miracle. We started talking about girls, drugs, and rock and roll, but the Holy Spirit changed the subject to Jesus. He took an ordinary, rebellious action and created a mystery. It became very clear to me that "God's ways are not our ways." God really is a God of mystery.

The role of youth ministry is to bring teenagers into the presence of a God who is beyond words, definition, or confinement; to create opportunities for teenagers to be awed by God's presence and stunned by God's bigness; and to show them a God who will leave them speechless, full of wonder and astonishment. Youth workers introduce students to a God who is more than principles and answers—we bring teenagers to the "shores of mystery."

Here are a few practical suggestions.

Questions, not answers

Here's a question from letter to God written by a little girl, "Dear God, are you really invisible or is that just a trick?"

Good question. In fact, the magic and fun of childhood come from questions like this. When we were children, we barraged adults and friends with questions, which were symptoms of our curiosity. Somewhere between being a child and becoming a "grown-up," we lost our inquisitiveness. We lost our curiosity and were satisfied with not knowing. This is what happens in the development of a secular culture. It is not the death of God; it is the

I believe that while "questions are more important than answers," there has to be a time when we can share with our students some of the answers we've discovered in our own spiritual journeys. The only problem is that the older I get and the more things I experience, the more questions I have. As I grow and learn, what I thought I knew about students and how to minister to them is challenged, so I have to ask more questions. Most wise people I know seem to have a good grasp of how much there is to know and how little of it they really know themselves.

—*Dave Ambrose*

death of questions about God. Because it thinks it has him all figured out, culture is no longer interested in God. When we abandon questions to live only in the world of answers, we have squashed the Holy Spirit in our lives.

Inquisitiveness, curiosity, the love of questions, comes from three sources: surprise, desire, and pain.

1. **Surprise.** Surprise is some combination of astonishment, amazement, wonder, and shock. Throughout the Bible, God seems to work best by surprises. He surprised Adam and Eve in the garden; Moses at the burning bush; Shadrach, Meshach, and Abednego in the fire; Jonah with the big fish; Abraham and Sarah with her pregnancy; Goliath with David; Paul on the road to Damascus; and Peter through his dreams. In fact, the disciples spent much of their three years with Jesus surprised. Jesus would show up in the oddest of places, at the strangest times, and with the most unusual people: at weddings, during storms on lakes, on the water without a boat, and with a lot of questionable women. The disciples were constantly amazed. Jesus even showed up after he had died.

There is something about being ambushed by God that increases our awe of him, our amazement at who he is and what he does. It is the unexpectedness of God that makes the mystery of him even more mysterious, and a good youth ministry finds ways to introduce students to the surprising God, giving them the opportunity to be bushwhacked by the God of the universe.

If you want more ideas for creating an atmosphere in which God can surprise students, check out Youth Specialties' Soul Shaper line of resources.

2. Desire. Desire has been given a bum rap. Because of guilt by association, it has a sleazy reputation. People associate desire with sex, lust, and erotic passion, so most students (and many older ones) think two things about desire:

a. Desire is bad.

b. Desire is ungodly.

This is too bad, because true desire couldn't be further from its reputation. Even though the word does hang around a bad crowd sometimes, it actually has great meaning and power in the Christian life.

Rarely do people in youth groups talk about desire positively. Mostly we talk about evil desires, unhealthy desires, and desires of the flesh. This, of course, is important, but not as important as talking about our desire for God. In some cases we do talk about a

> Because of the distorted way the church has often defined desire, a lot of students I know have developed a disdain for their desires as though they were the enemies—"If only I didn't need to be loved so much, I wouldn't be so weak in my relationships..."; "If I could only get over my need to get approval, I wouldn't be so driven in and obsessed with everything I do." As Mike says so clearly, much of the thirst we experience in life is God-given and is, in fact, designed to draw us toward him.
>
> The problem is not the desire but my sinful predisposition to satisfy my desires in unhealthy and relationally destructive ways. I demand that my thirst be quenched on my terms and according my timetable. It's so important for me to stay in charge. In the lives of my students, I see the pattern of my life—and we've got it all backward. Desire doesn't make us sinful; our sinfulness misdirects desire.
>
> —*Marv Penner*

positive form of desire; we talk about loving God and desiring good, justice, and mercy. In effect, though, this reduces desire to something that can be controlled and used. Our desire for God is very different. We can't control godly desire. It's just there, and sometimes it happens when we least expect it. We can't control what form it will take or when it will show up, but we can respond to it, we can listen to it, and we can pay attention to it. We won't, however, always understand it. This is the important point: *our desire for God and the longings that come with our desire are great mysteries.*

This is a mystery because becoming aware of our godly

desires brings us face to face with God himself. The longings I have for meaning, for hope, for security, for significance, for relationship, and for forgiveness are symptoms of God's imprint on my soul.

People throughout the Bible experience this innate longing. In John 4, Jesus begins a conversation with a woman by a well. This woman knows all about physical desire—she's been married five times and is living with the man who might become number six. Apparently out of the blue, Jesus tells the woman he can give her living water. Here's the amazing thing: *the woman wants the living water*. It's not clear if she understands exactly what Jesus is talking about, but somewhere inside she can feel a stirring. Realizing this is no ordinary person, she begins to sense this man has something to do with God. Her desire for God is awakened, and she begins to ask her friends, "Is this the Christ?" Because she felt the stirring of her natural desire for God, she connected with Jesus. She is stunned by him and becomes an evangelist in seconds.

When we help teenagers get in touch with their desire for living water, they will want to know more. There will be a stirring inside of them, and they will ask questions, perhaps the same question as the woman at the well. Then they will see Jesus. How this works is a mystery, but it does.

3. **Pain.** Youth groups are not supposed to be sanctuaries of pain (we don't include it on our list in chapter seven). Youth ministry is not about inflicting pain and penance on kids; it is about identifying Jesus in the midst of pain and suffering. Although youth groups can be places where students participate in fun activities

---

One of our CORE values is that *discomfort is better than comfort*, which sounds as if we're a little cruel. But it's not so much that we're saying comfort is a bad thing; it's just that discomfort keeps us in pursuit of better things. One says, "I've arrived," and the other says, "I'm pressing on." Many students get so comfortable with biblical truth that they cease to grow; they cease to move forward. That's why, sometimes, the only route to deeper joy is through greater pain.

—Duffy Robbins

and have great experiences, it does not mean youth workers can ignore the value of suffering when it comes. Youth group is not a hospital where we fix our students' pain and protect them from suffering; it is a holy place where we help teenagers recognize God, even in their suffering. We should allow students to struggle, to work out their own salvation, to seek God when they can't feel him, and support them through it.

There is constant struggle in the Christian life because Christianity is not only about living and life; it's also about dying and death. We die to self, yes, and we also have to die many other deaths, which is why Jesus came. It's great to talk to kids about happiness, joy, and life, but we must also talk about giving up, letting go, and death. God will meet them there, too.

What keeps our teenagers from experiencing the wild, erotic presence of God is not alcohol and drugs. It's the narcotic effect of comfort and familiarity, of safety. When people feel safe, they are stagnant; there is no pain, no death, and no life. Jesus did not say, "I have come to give you safety and to give you safety more abundantly." Jesus came to give us life *and* a sword. He makes it very clear that "whoever finds his life will lose it, and whoever loses his life for my sake will find it" (Matthew 10:39).

Simple *and* complicated

What is simple and complicated? The body—it has many parts, but is one unit (1 Corinthians 12:12-31). What is simple and complicated? The wind—it blows where it pleases, but we cannot tell where it comes from or where it goes (John 3:8). What is simple and complicated? Love—"Now we

What is simple and complicated? How about youth ministry! Constantly I need to remind myself that youth ministry is not a formula or an equation. Things don't always turn out the way we plan. We can set up programs with all the "right" ingredients, spend time in prayer, and go in believing God will do great things, and...nothing. What happened? It's a mystery. Or we throw an event together at the last minute, go in with a bad attitude, and wish for the evening to end so we can go home, and God shows up in a big way—the place is thick with his presence. Why? It's a mystery!

—*Tic Long*

see but a poor reflection as in a mirror; then we shall see face to face. Now I know in part; then I shall know fully, even as I am fully known" (1 Corinthians 13:12), and we shall be loved perfectly. These simple, basic truths of God point to a mystery far beyond our comprehension.

Because we want our students to comprehend the Bible, to understand Christianity, it is an easy temptation for us to take complicated truth and make it simplistic. Often youth workers reduce complicated truth to slogans or formulas that are easier to understand, but this diminishes the gospel. *Awesome*, as in "Our God is an awesome God," is a great word, but God is far more than awesome. He is terrifying, threatening, and consuming. He is something way beyond our wildest imaginations, and it's important that we tell teenagers this from the very beginning. God is awesome, but he's also mysterious. God is knowable, but he's also invisible. God is our father, but he's also our king.

Because this is hard, because we can't understand the complexities of God and his word, we push the complicated concepts into simplified phrases and principles. The will of God is one mystery that we like to simplify. Instead of calling it God's will, we say "plan," and we convince students that God has a plan, a specific plan for each and every one of us: one person to marry, one prefect job, a specific number of children, a certain time to die. But maybe God doesn't have a detailed day-by-day plan for each of us; maybe our job is to seek God's presence rather than which conference he wants us to attend. Maybe we should be looking for God rather than a map for our lives. We'd rather not get into an argument here because the will of God is complicated (as are most subjects relating to God), and we must be careful not to uncomplicate it by making it clean and easy. It isn't. It is in the complicated things of life where we really experience the mystery of God.

We also simplify what is complex when we make conclusions about people and their faith without knowing the whole story. Faith is simply, "I believe," but each person's faith is a complex combination of many layers and dimensions. This is hard to grasp and difficult to fit into our understanding of faith, so we reduce other people's faith to one layer, one dimension. However, we are all much more complicated than what people see. We have histories, experiences, and emotions that others can't see.

Here's an example of a couple whose faith was simplified by others who were later shocked to learn how complicated that couple's life had been.

Sarah had died in the prime of her life. She was staggeringly beautiful and, having just finished her college education, was beginning a life filled with promise. Everyone liked Sarah and knew that her faith was an important part of her life. The accident had been so quick, so senseless, so unfair, so devastatingly final. Sarah, driving home from work, hit the freeway abutment at 70 miles an hour. To this day no one knows why or how it happened. All the family knows is that it did happen. Their daughter, gone in an instant, no time for good-byes, no time to prepare.

Sarah's parents were Christians. They prayed daily, were active in their church, and supported many outside ministries. Their home had been a haven for troubled youth looking for someone who cared and understood; Daryl and Kara had been a dad and mom to countless teenagers, walking through many struggles with them: divorce, cancer, suicide, and depression.

And now it was their turn. The light of their life was snuffed out, and they would be forced to sit in the church with family and friends and say good-bye to their daughter. They would have to try to find the words to comfort, try to find the strength to endure, try to find the resources to cope with a loss beyond words.

It was a powerful service, and the most powerful moment was when Sarah's parents stood to say a few words. In the stunned silence, the crowd of several hundred marveled at the carefully worded tribute given by Sarah's parents. They spoke of faith and its power to carry one through a loss like this; they talked of the hope that comes from trusting God in moments of darkness; they celebrated their daughter's own faith in God and encouraged other students to have a relationship with God. When the broken couple sat down, most people were crying, and everyone was deeply moved by the strength and courage of the grieving parents. What amazing faith! It seemed their faith could help everyone live happily ever after. But it was more complex than that.

Within six months Sarah's parents had filed for divorce, their son had moved out of the house, vowing never to return and refusing to speak to the parents. Both parents were in counseling and on antidepression medication. Neither parent attended church regularly. Currently, however, both periodically visit various churches trying to make their way back to the faith they once had.

How do we explain what happened here? The students who witnessed the funeral left convinced that Sarah's parents' faith was solid as a rock, but it wasn't. What happened to their faith? Did it just disappear, swallowed up in grief and despair? Did their rational understanding of their relationship with God simply break apart when they were faced with the illogical death of an innocent girl? How do we make sense of a family who appeared to have a strong and hope-filled faith when it collapses into a tangle of hopelessness and despair?

We may not be able to make sense of it. It may remain a mystery, but we can understand that it happened because the real Daryl and Kara were much more complicated than they appeared. While everyone saw two rock-solid parents grieving the loss of their daughter, in truth they weren't rock-solid at all. Their marriage had been in trouble for years; their relationship was strained already, and communication had ceased years ago. This couple wasn't hiding their dysfunction; they weren't consciously living a secret life that they carefully hid from everyone else. They were a normal couple that knew their relationship was in trouble, who recognized the decay of their marriage, and who honestly believed one day they would sit down together and work through their difficulties. But they had children to raise, jobs to perform, church activities to attend, places to go, things to do. Without realizing it, more than a few days passed before they could sit down to talk— years went by, then a decade or two, and then a tragedy exposed all of the problems they had postponed. Now they had to deal with them.

Daryl and Kara hadn't shown this complexity to others for years. Were they honest people? Yes. Were they good people? Yes. But they were also complicated, as we all are. This is not about blaming Sarah's parents; it is a matter of understanding how difficult real life is. People are complex, and their faiths are complex.

This is part of the mystery of God and the mystery of faith. Faith may not always cushion the blow, but God will always be with us. We want to be a part of God's will, but we won't always know what that means. We want to know God, but we don't always feel him. It is simple and complex. That is the mystery of faith.

Presence, not program

The key word is *presence*. What can and will have a deep and lasting impact on our students is a powerful experience of the presence of God. We spend hours talking to our students about the implications of believing in God; we spend even more hours talking about God, but we spend very little time creating the opportunity for them to experience the mystery of God in his presence. Only recently has it occurred to those of us in youth ministry that maybe our focus should change from programs about God to experiences with God. Here are some ways that we can create spaces for God experiences.

The Matthew 25:31-46 experience. The more our students hang out with the poor and serve the hungry, the more they come in contact with Jesus. Jesus made it very clear that he is present in the poor and the suffering. Strange as it may seem, teenagers can meet Jesus for the first time in the dump in Mexico. They can meet him in our church buildings, too, but sometimes they see him more clearly in the barrio. This is a part of the mystery of Jesus—we find him in the most unlikely places.

Spiritual exercise experiences. There are many ways to pray, many spiritual exercises we can use to sense the presence of Jesus. Youth workers can find numerous resources that offer a variety of prayer exercises that enable students to pay attention to God's

During our end-of-junior-high trip, all the students are required to give testimonies of their faith. We encourage them to be authentic and specific. Typically the testimonies begin, "I grew up in a Christian home and accepted Christ when I was 3 1/2 years old..." One year, though, toward the end of the testimonies, Ted stood to give his. In about six minutes he genuinely explained that he had not yet put his faith in Christ and wasn't sure if he would do it. At this point looks of shock and anxiety spread across the faces of my other students. Immediately following our session, many came up to me and said, "We have to do something! Should we all write him notes?" They wanted so much to fix Ted.

Instead of starting a letter-writing campaign, I encouraged them to do what they were already doing—loving and accepting Ted and letting Christ's light shine through them, to be present for him so he could experience God's presence. "That's it?" they asked. "Yep."

God is still working on Ted, and my kids are still working to let God work on Ted.

—*Heather Flies*

presence. And, of course, there is the labyrinth, which is becoming more and more a fixture of ministry. It simply creates a silent opportunity for students to venture into the mysterious depths of their own souls accompanied by Jesus.

CORE Reality: Mystery

In *The Horse and His Boy* from C.S. Lewis' incomparable Chronicles of Narnia, Shasta, a young boy, is lost, tired, and alone. He was beginning to feel sorry for himself when he "discovered that someone or somebody was walking beside him. It was pitch dark and he could see nothing. And the Thing (or Person) was going so quietly that he could hardly hear any footfalls. What he could hear was breathing. His invisible companion seemed to breathe on a very large scale, and Shasta got the impression that it was a very large creature."

But just when he thought he was imagining it all, "there suddenly came a deep, rich sigh out of the darkness beside him. That couldn't be imagination! Anyway, he had felt the hot breath of that sigh on his chilly left hand."

After a rather lengthy conversation with his unseen companion, Shasta "was no longer afraid that the Voice belonged to something that could eat him, nor that it was the voice of a ghost. *But a new and different trembling came over him. Yet he felt glad too*" (Collier, 1954. p. 159).

Trembling and gladness are not bad goals for youth ministry. We are convinced that the only thing our students need when they graduate from our ministries is the life-changing memory of the time they spent with *the one* who can breathe on a very large scale, *the one* who took on the very nature of a servant, *the one* who humbled himself, *the one* who was given the name above all names, the mysterious Son of God.

MANDATE: Youth ministry must foster mystery, rediscover astonishment, and leave room for unanswered questions.

CHAPTER TEN

CORE REALITY

CREATIVITY

GENESIS 1:26-27

2 CORINTHIANS 5:17

JOEL 2:28

EXODUS 34:10

Mike's Story

Every year our youth group traveled with a few other groups to Mexico to build houses for the poor. One of the youth groups we traveled with was from Beverly Hills, a very expensive place to live. As part of its annual fundraising to pay for the houses, the Beverly Hills youth group sponsored an auction. Because it was located in Beverly Hills, this was no ordinary auction. People were asked to donate expensive items, and they did. One year the Beverly Hills youth group's fundraising goal was $22,000. One student was determined to raise the most money for the auction. He was bright, direct, a bit nerdy, and not intimidated by adults. We'll call him Henry.

Henry walked into the most exclusive bank in Beverly Hills and asked for the president. After giving him the coldest of stares, the receptionist sent Henry to the bank president's secretary. Unfazed, he asked, "Could I talk to the president for a few minutes?" Barely acknowledging his presence, the secretary said, "He's busy. Very busy."

"That's okay," Henry said, "I've got the rest of the day. I'll wait."

He waited for a couple of hours before the secretary came to Henry in a huff: "He said he has two minutes, but he's very busy."

As Henry walked into the president's massive and intimidating office, the president looked the boy up and down and said in a slightly irritated voice, "What can I do for you?"

"Well, I'm from Hollywood High School, and I—"

The president interrupted, "Hollywood High School? I graduated from there. Is Miss Granville still there and still a miss?"

"Uh, actually she is."

"Well, how about that? Well, what can I do for you, son? I imagine you're raising money for something. Will a hundred dollars do?"

"Actually I was wondering if the bank owned a condo."

Taken aback, the president responded warily, "Yes, we do."

"I was wondering if you would be willing to give us one week at your condo to auction in order to raise money to build houses for the poor in Mexico." The bank president was so impressed, he said yes and determined which week the condo would be available.

As the boy was leaving, the bank president said, "By the way, can you accept cash?"

"Sure," Henry said confidently. The bank president sat down, wrote a check, and handed it to Henry. It was for $3,000.

Most kids would have been blown away and run back to the church to celebrate the good news. Not Henry. He was on a mission. Walking down the street to the next bank he could find, he entered and asked for the president. When the president finally met with him, Henry said, "We're raising money to build houses for the poor in Mexico. The bank down the street gave us $3,000. What are you going to do?" He walked out of that bank with a check for $1,000.

In one afternoon Henry raised $4,000 in cash and a week at a condo that was auctioned for $2,000. Henry was creative. His ingenuity and courage had taken the bank presidents by surprise, and they responded. Henry didn't do fundraising the way it had always been done, and as a result, six families in Mexico now have homes of their own.

Creativity is the ability to bring into existence something new by using one's imagination, ingenuity, and inventiveness. Because we are made in the image of God, the God who invented creativity, we are creative as well—*all of us*. Youth ministry must help teenagers rediscover their creativity. The youth group should be known for its inventiveness, imagination, and ingenuity. It should be the breeding place of wonder, passion, and unpredictability. So to incorporate and develop creativity in our programs, we must know what kinds of creativity there are, what the enemies of creativity are, and what we can do to foster it in ourselves and in our students.

Types of creativity

Only God can create something out of nothing, so rather than create something out of nothing, we create something out of something. We're more limited, so our creativity involves revisioning, copying, and adapting, the three basic kinds of creativity.

Revisioning. Rarely, if ever, does someone create something new. Even Einstein's theory of relativity discovered what was already there. But Einstein saw what others couldn't see; he saw the facts in a new way. He invented a new way of looking at how the world works—a *re*-vision. Revisioning is a re-seeing—seeing something in a new light or from a completely different

> As "made in God's image" creatures, we are *all* creative—no theological way around that. But I find that so many think creativity demands an *ex nihilo* magic, a new thing out of nothing (like God's creation of the world). Not so, fellow creative creatures! Most of the best creativity in youth ministry comes from modifying, tweaking, and customizing existing ideas to meet the specific needs of your students.
>
> —*Mark Oestreicher*

angle. When we look at our youth programs and the problems in our churches differently, when we revision them, then we can find new ways of ministering that can knock the socks off our kids and our congregations.

When students complain that youth group is boring, the solution may become apparent when we see that the problem isn't that the meetings are boring but that the students don't understand what we're saying and get bored. When the church complains that kids skating in the parking lot is a problem, we might be able to see that the skating isn't a problem, but the insurance is. Then we might be able to find a creative solution.

One group we know started a boxing club and Bible study. The Bible study was part of the discipline of being a fighter, and God continues to use this powerful ministry. Another youth worker developed a racing team to build and race cars in the local racing circuit. What great ways to revision youth group activities!

Copying. For most of us copying as creativity shows up in our ministries. We hear about a new way of doing a Bible study, and we try it. There is nothing wrong with copying. If it's new for our groups, it's creative. When my youth group traveled to Mexico each year for work camps, on-site food preparation was a problem. One man in our community decided, on his own, to solve our problem. After gutting an old travel trailer, he rebuilt it with a propane stove, refrigerator, water system, and storage space for dishes and utensils. A self-contained cooking trailer was not his idea; he had seen one the year before while we were at our work camp in Mexico, and he copied the idea. But his cooking trailer was creative for us.

Adapting. Brainstorming is the process of taking what we already know and rearranging it for a different situation. Creativity takes what we already know, adapts it, and puts it in a new setting. Something new has been created from something old. When I first started in youth ministry, the other leaders and I were trying to create a new way of doing evangelism. We wanted to find creative ways of attracting a crowd of teenagers to an event where we could present the gospel in a new way. What we came up with was a hayride (an old idea) but with a modern twist (adapted). In order to update this old idea and make it more attractive to teens, we decided to call it "the world's largest hayride" and haul kids around with 18-wheeler trucks covered with hay. Instead of driving around in the hills, though, we decided to have the hayride downtown and drive through the city. We couldn't believe how many high school students turned up—1,300! Something we hadn't counted on was the police coverage. They pointed out that 1,300 teenagers throwing hay over the road and at other cars was a problem, so we spent all night on the world's largest cleanup. Because of insurance issues and SUVs, this probably wouldn't be possible today, but this (now old) idea can be creatively adapted.

Enemies of creativity

Creativity can affect everything we do in our youth groups—games, activities, meetings, content, camps, Bible studies, worship, church. By altering what we do, by giving new life to the old, we can get teenagers excited and involved in making the youth group their own, different from anyone else's. But there's a problem we have to face. Not everybody welcomes creativity. There are enemies out there.

Most churches are thrilled to have nice, predictable, comfortable youth groups where students are happily involved in the activities, growing in numbers, and satisfied with the programs. Youth workers are supposed to teach teenagers what to believe and how to act so that when they are older, they will not depart from their faith—nice, predictable, comfortable youth groups. What churches don't want is trouble. What they don't want is risk. Most churches will support creativity in the youth group...*as long as it isn't too creative.*

Creativity sounds like a nice idea, but when it meddles with our comfort level, when it disturbs our long-held beliefs, when it interferes with our worldviews or threatens our values, then we're not too sure. It's scary. The religious leaders were afraid of Jesus; they had no problem with him as long as he would stay in the Messiah box they had created, as long as he would do what they thought a Messiah should do. As long as Jesus didn't break the rules, trample over the entrenched religious laws, or challenge their image of God, the religious leaders were happy to let him lead his merry band of followers.

But that is exactly what Jesus did. He was creative, inventive, and unpredictable. As a result he created enemies. But if you think the church and the world are ready to welcome creativity the way Christ was creative, think again. Creativity threatens the status quo and disrupts those who are comfortable. *But creativity also attracts the unattractive, reaches the unreachable, converts the unconverted, brings healing to the unhealable, sight to the blind, and health to the unhealthy.* Unfortunately, this is what troubles most people about creativity, and they create obstacles. Between these and the daily obstacles we meet, creativity can be squelched. However, if you are aware of the dangers of too much reliance on numbers, reducing God to rules, bad theology, technological dependence, and fear, staying creative will be easier.

Measurements. *Counting* and *measuring* are tyrants that can smother creativity. People and church boards obsessed with measuring have little tolerance for that which cannot be charted, compared, and increased. Many youth workers have taken over a youth group in which 95 percent of the program is centered on fun and games. If a youth worker in this situation decides to change the focus of the group to Bible study, small groups, or worship, kids who were used to playing all the time complain and drop out. As a result, the numbers drop, the complaints increase, and that youth worker can get pressured to return the program to the way it was. However, what couldn't be measured in that change were the types of people who were reached, the quality of the relationships with God that were developed, and the level of commitment to Jesus among the students who stayed.

Reductionism. This is a fancy word for boiling down all of life to a set of principles or laws that, if followed, are guaranteed to produce results. For example, if you read your Bible every day and have quiet time, your relationship with Jesus will be close and your life will be more committed. Although there's nothing wrong with wanting to study the Bible daily, such a habit doesn't guarantee anything. So it doesn't make much sense to make it a rule of religious life that every Christian must spend 30 minutes every morning, before leaving the house, reading his or her Bible. The Pharisees had rules like this; they prayed and read the Torah daily, but it didn't change their lives. If we reduce the Christian life to a set of rules and principles, then we leave no room for other possibilities, other places where God can work in our lives. It may be, for some of us who live on the coast, that walking the beach daily makes a huge difference in our relationships with God, more so than spending 30 minutes every morning looking at the pages of the Bible.

One young student was told she needed to decide between following God and dancing, that she couldn't do both. The Christian life had been reduced to one that couldn't involve dance; God had been reduced to a god who wouldn't work through dance. This advice couldn't have been more wrong in her case. Dancing was the way she connected with God. Dancing was her way of communicating with God what couldn't be said with words, and because God honors creativity, he honored her dancing; he would not be reduced. Reductionism stifles creativity because it limits God. Creativity opens all the avenues to God and gives us unlimited access to God. Creativity allows us to meet God where we never imagined he would be.

Bad theology. To some, creativity is a sin. According to these folks, what was good enough for Paul should be good enough for us. They are suspicious of anything new and always worry that new means liberal. Throughout the Bible it's God who constantly forces the religious people to recognize the newness of life, the fresh wind of the Holy Spirit. God used rocks, sticks, mud, water, furnaces, lions, fish, fire, earthquakes, wind, writing on a wall, donkeys, slingshots, perfume, snakes, wine, sheep, money, fig trees, wheat, seeds, pigs, frogs, locusts, and prostitutes. And we've just described the tip of the iceberg! Continually, God changed the types of people through whom he spoke and the ways in which his message was communicated. So when people believe God works only one way, they have bad theology. When God works, there is no limit to his creativity. God can communicate through anything or anyone.

Technology. This is not an anti-technology rant. We are pro-technology, and much of today's technology was developed because people were creative. It can even assist people (the younger generation especially) in expressing their creativity. Because they have grown up with cell phones, DVDs, computers, video games, and the Internet, technology is enmeshed in the lives of our

> We were on an Ecuador mission trip a few years ago when one of my students reminded me how ingenious teenagers can be. Our task was to paint the roof of a Missionary Aviation Airport hangar. We took a compressed-air paint-spraying machine with us. Because we were so far back in the jungle and there was no way to get replacement parts, we kept praying that this machine would keep working. Sure enough, a couple of days into our work, the machine broke; a washer cracked and paint was seeping from the machine. Technology had failed us. What were we supposed to do now?
>
> We searched for an extra washer with absolutely no luck. Then one of my students asked if he could have a button from the shirt of one of the men working with us. He cut the button off the man's shirt, walked to the drill press, and drilled a small hole in the middle of the button. We watched him as he walked over to the paint machine and replaced the broken washer with the "button washer" he had just made. We had been lulled by technology into thinking that only mechanical parts would work. But we were wrong. That machine kept working without skipping a beat for the rest of the week, and we were able to complete our job thanks to the ingenuity and creativity of one student who was not limited by technology!
>
> —*Dave Ambrose*

kids. But don't confuse new technology with creativity. Technology may be the result of creativity, but it does not necessarily foster creativity. Often technology leads to *dependency*. First a few of us had cell phones; then everyone had them; now we are dependent on them. Technology can swallow any available time and energy we have because it engages all of our faculties, so we have none left to think creatively. If we aren't aware of the deadening effects of technology, it can consume every second of leisure we have, every minute we could be developing creative ideas. We are not against technology; we are wary of it and cautious when using it.

Fear. Creativity is often stymied by our own insecurities and fears—fears of failure, ridicule, criticism. By worrying about the implications or results of our creativity, we interrupt or shut down the creative juices because we keep checking to make sure there are no negative results. This is much like the little boy who planted an onion plant is his garden, and once the leaves came through the ground, he kept yanking the plant out of the ground to see if it was growing. Of course it died. If, fearing rejection, we keep interrupting our creativity to monitor how it will be received, we will kill our creativity.

These obstacles might trip us as we try to develop creative youth ministry programs. Some are especially tricky because they are not innately bad. However, they can become obstacles. If we are aware of them, though, and keep in mind the different types of creativity, then we are on our way to creating exciting new ministries. But implementing these creative ideas into our programs can be difficult.

Methods of fostering creativity

In order to create an atmosphere in which creativity can happen in our youth ministry, we must believe in the power of creativity, trust our creative abilities, refuse to give in to those who don't, include our students in the processes, and keep our focus on our ministries.

1. **Believe in creativity.** Seriously. Put it on the radar; make it a priority. Although many youth workers plan fun activities with their students, thinking creatively never enters their minds. They don't spend much time looking for new ways to do things; they might be looking for better ways to do what they've always done, and this involves some creativity, but new elements, ones that approach the program from a completely different angle, add life to it.

2. **Trust your uniqueness.** We've said this before in chapter three, and it's important to mention it again. Why should you trust your uniqueness? Because what makes you different is the result of God's creativity. Each one of us is different, individual, unique, so each one of us has different gifts, weaknesses, and specialties. Also, each one of us has a different youth group with its own needs and strengths. Many youth ministries are franchised or

I was the full-time youth minister at a church in Fullerton, California, for 22 years and was fortunate enough to meet a lot of wonderful volunteers who worked on our staff. One of the most memorable was a man named Forrest Bright. Forrest worked with his hands most of his life. A carpenter by trade, he had built some fine homes in our area, and I admired him before I really knew him. He was a quiet man who, on the weekends, would do odd repair and construction jobs for single moms in our church.

One day he asked if he could work with the youth, but he did not want to stand in front of a group and speak, nor did he want to lead a small group of students in a discussion. Yet, in some way, he felt God calling him to work with teenagers.

I asked if he would allow some of them to assist him on the weekends when he did repairs for those in need. He agreed, and for the next two years, he had several young men and a few young women help him. Some even went on to become journeyman carpenters themselves. I think they learned more from Forrest in one weekend than they did from a dozen of my talks. They watched this large, gentle man with a big heart minister to people. God used Forrest's abilities to provide a creative ministry for the students as well as those they helped.

You may not know Forrest, but I bet you know about his younger brother—Bill Bright founded Campus Crusade for Christ. While the success of Bill's ministry is undeniable, I've always admired how Forrest used the gifts and creativity God had given to him. Sometimes I wonder who really had the most successful ministry!

—*Les Christie*

copied, and that is a great place to start. But to allow our creativity to work, we need to recognize our own unique qualities because our individual perspectives and gifts make our ministries a true reflection of the Holy Spirit in us.

3. **Refuse to give in to the Creative Police**. The Creative Police are the naysayers, the lawsuit worriers, the insurance monitors, the it-can't-be-done-ers. These people will tell you they want you to be creative *but*…Find people who will help you implement your creative ideas responsibly and beware of the many who are afraid to try them at all. Jesus taught his disciples to become people who were willing to try new ways of ministry, eager to see the law in a new light, and ready to use trial and error putting these new ideas into practice.

The church says it believes in Jesus and wants students to know Jesus, but when it comes to using the methods of Jesus and his disciples, it sometimes balks. The church itself often acts as the long arm of the Creative Police. If we want teenagers to follow Jesus, though, they have to follow him everywhere—into the temple while he turns over the tables, into the wedding where he makes wine, into a group of angry people who are ready to kill an adulterous woman. Creativity is the way of Jesus, and it is the way of youth ministry as well.

4. **Exercise your students' imagination.** Learn the art of creative thinking—revisioning, copying, and adapting—and ask your students to do the same. To think differently, to think in a new way.

That's right—creativity as a CORE reality isn't just about *your* creativity! It's a biblical reality that we also see our students as creative beings, made in the image of a super-creative God! We need to be passionate about fanning the flame of their creativity, stoking the fires of their dreams, developing the space for their explorations!

—Mark Oestreicher

Encourage change. Every time you do a Bible study, take time to allow kids to imagine themselves in the stories. Encourage them to use art, drama, movement, and music as much as possible. Allow them to create plays, raps, limericks, and poems to exercise their imaginations. Encourage them to use their skills in new ways, to contribute to the youth group in ways they haven't before. Help them to recognize the creative power of the Holy Spirit within themselves—you might even get an idea or five from them.

5. **Keep your focus on your ministry.** Creativity can be distracting as well as enhancing. Youth workers should not be creative for creativity's sake. Creativity is not an end in itself. It is not a novelty or an attempt to impress others. Usually, ideas developed without any goal in mind simply because they're creative don't work well. The purpose of creativity is to make what we're doing or saying more helpful, useful, and effective. Our goal in youth ministry is to make our ministries more effective, so our creative ideas should always be focused on our ministries. If the new ideas do not address the needs of our groups, then it doesn't matter how creatively they have been adapted because they haven't

achieved the goal—in fact, the purpose—of creativity. We should be clever, ingenious, and creative, and the question motivating our creativity should always be, *"How do I make my ministry more effective?"*

CORE Reality: Creativity

Creativity is the footprint God leaves on his children—on us and on our students—so creativity is one of the CORE realities of an effective youth ministry. However, one must be vigilant because people and cultures that forget about God forget about creativity, too. They forget to listen and watch for the powerful wind of the Holy Spirit. They forget that their own creativity is a mark of their maker. In fact, one of the characteristics of a pagan culture is the demise of creativity. There is no secular or pagan conspiracy against creativity; rather society slowly convinces us to give up trying, to give up experimenting. Before we realize what's happened to us, our creative, childlike imagination is dead, and we no longer have the courage to be creative.

We have no limitations and nothing to fear because we have God's support: "I can do everything through him who gives me strength" (Philippians 4:13). Not only do we have his support, but Jesus has already helped us to succeed: "We are more than conquerors through him who loved us" (Romans 8:37). We have the strength given to us from the very God who created creativity, so we can shout, "YES! Of course I can!"

MANDATE: Youth ministry must free students and youth workers to discover and express their God-given creativity.

A collection of truth in the form of
stories overflowing with **anecdotes, confessions,** and
conversations about **renewal, salvation,**
and **revelations** that **ignite lively sessions** and
expose life-affirming answers

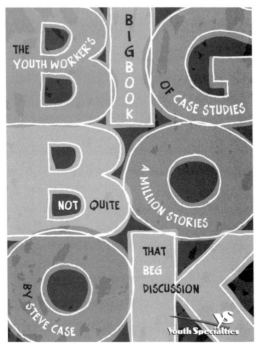

Softcover   ISBN 0310-25562-7

Honest. Genuine.
Field-tested.

Three of your favorites from Mike Yaconelli!

Softcover	60-minute video	Softcover
0-310-23533-2	0-310-23878-1	1576-83128-0

"Yaconelli has an annoying habit of speaking the truth."
—Publishers Weekly on *Messy Spirituality*

"He makes you step back and think while being inspirational and fun."
—Youthworker on *Youth Ministry Outside the Lines*

"The book is suffused with a humanness—a broken honesty"
—Group on *Dangerous Wonder*

To order these and other resources written by Mike Yaconelli
Visit **www.youthspecialties.com/store** or visit your local Christian bookstore